SKINNY
DIPPING
IN
DAYLIGHT

Skinny Dipping in Daylight
Published by
Fog Ink, an imprint of
Fields of Gold Publishing, Inc.
in conjunction with
The Raven and the Writing Desk

For information contact:
The Raven & The Writing Desk
311 N. Margin St
Franklin, TN 37064.

Editor: Melissa Wyllie
Cover design & all illustrations: Cory Basil
hereliescorybasil.com

ISBN: 978-0-9990104-0-2

SKINNY

DIPPING

IN

DAYLIGHT

CORY BASIL

THE RAVEN AND THE WRITING DESK

&

FOG INK PUBLISHING

NASHVILLE, TENNESSEE

INTRODUCTION

 WAS TOLD BY A FRIEND THAT PO-
etry was dead. Not poetry itself, but
the art of writing, the soul of the
craft, it was as she said it, "missing
in action." I myself have written
four collections of poetry. All of them in various stages
and degrees of expression, exploration and examination.
Not all of them have been published, and the ones that
have didn't sell in any great mass. But that never stopped
me from continuing the great exercise of writing, reading
and buying poetry. In fact, it is this very same passion for
the art that has led me to writing this forward for my
great friend and peer, Cory Basil.

Poetry is far from dead, it just needs to be brought
back out into the light. Yes, I do agree that the old Mas-
ters will continue to rattle around our dusty shelves or
cobwebbed archives online. But the new poets, the new

blood, they need the same kind of reassurance and exultation that the old ones had.

"Every Poet should be fed by Ravens." This thought has always hounded me, because it rings true. I think poets should suffer for their art, dig deep into the canals of buried treasure and unearth all its secrets in front of us, dripping of ancient unbridled mysteries. But the suffering should also reap reward, and by reading and embracing the new poets we give them back their voice. Cory Basil is the newest voice of poetry. It is simple, and it is plain and it is also truth in obscurity, unrelenting honesty and tortured revelations. In this book, he speaks of coming face-to-face with his own frailty, but also the supernatural desire to change himself in the process. He speaks of churches, vampires, love and lust. He speaks of loss, lamentations but also the beauty in every little detail. For that is it, that is the apex of all great poetry, it is the illumination of the smallest detail that makes us take notice of our lives.

We are not dead, and neither is the great Art.

— Kevin Max
author of *At the Foot of Heaven* and *Unfinished Work*

FROM THE AUTHOR

S I WALKED ACROSS THE BONES OF my memories I could see that each of these dead things held their own simple beauty. Amongst their decaying skin lying in the soil of my years were etchings of moments that if I let sink to be buried beneath would be lost forever. The seasons of the soul and spirit do not follow those of the solstice and equinox, yet hold steadfast to a mysterious movement that mankind will never come to define. It is these seasons and these dead things I have saved from the destruction of personal deletion. For it is far simpler and much safer to throw them into the fire and numb all desire to understand the reasons why they ever came to be. Yet I have learned to walk across the bones of my memories and today I live with them in peace.

It has taken many years filled with countless secluded nights of sitting with pen and paper under low light to compose this collection, one I can only describe as a pure glimpse into my mind and into my life. I have left all as it was written in its time. As for some of the pieces, the pain speaks louder than correctly placing each line or perfecting each rhyme. The truth of that is more important to me than the prize of the other. There is an evolution that occurs within these pages, an evolution that was birthed by the shy quiet echo of my youth. A progression that will leave you having laid witness to a soul that has finally found its voice somewhere in the middle of life.

Herein lies a myriad medley containing the catharsis of the moment, thoughts emerging in the days following and reflections after the initial happening had long passed. This volume is my first footed foray into the mouth of the wolves. Sharpen your teeth little wolves, for my skin has grown quite thick.

— Cory Basil

CONTENTS

conversations on internal bleeding

love and everything below it

tiny arrows piercing the black

losing sight of the shore

across the bones of my memories

.

for the broken

CONVERSATIONS
ON
INTERNAL
BLEEDING

blue manifesto

i know what i need
needs me not
i know what i want
wants me not

i feel the pain
the pain i fought
i fought the feeling
of what i sought
i sought what i need
need sought me not
i sought what i want
want sought me not

i know what to do
to do what i ought
i know when to leave
leave what i ought

i shut off need
need claimed a lot
i shut off want
want stole a lot
need gave me nothing
but something to love
want gave me something
but nothing to love

i need something
want nothing
and have lost everything.

Web

What am I to do
With these memories of you
Feelings attached
Cold stale and blue
Flash to erase
Perhaps misplace
The thought of ever having
Or needing
You.

abandoned drifter

i bleed because it is all leaving
all fading away
just a shadow in the distance
nothing left to pray.
i fool myself into thinking
it could have all been so great
i feel myself disagreeing
that it was ever really fate.
i stagger through these streets
filling the world's gutter with my tears
pouring what's left of my soul
spilling my deepest fears.
the night is darker now
the space between others, more vast
my footsteps louder somehow
the fog seems to remain – to outlast.
heartache from the start
enough pain to fill every fiber, every string
every word spoken leaves its mark
every wound open – screaming.

back inside cold walls, still and silent
the only breath visible is mine
my heart dead – then racing
it's happening all the time.
understanding now the tricks of the mind
confusion, uncertainty – emotion, stress
heavy breathing and cold water
only these bring me back to digress.
seeing with eyes closed
clouds so thick, barely knowing you are there
uncertainty and troubles i never showed
if faith exists now i am unaware.
i must pen to let it escape
i have to get it all out
these thoughts my mind, they rape
caring not if others doubt.
have i not served my time
can you not show me the route
i am grasping for your hand
through thick air – through heavy cloud.

sober me up

i want to see it all so clearly now

light up my tunnel

spit me out of the whale.

part me a red sea

then show me dry land

raise oh please this dead man

birthed from out of the sand.

[22 january 2006. written at 3 a.m. – packing
what was left of what was once my home.]

Leave Me Be

What is this road I walk upon
Who are these creatures I meet
Some filled with love
Some confusion – some greed
Yet every face displays a need.

Love me today
Tomorrow I'll flee
Showcase of taste
No one to embrace
The simple man that is me.

The Haunting

Tonight I feel as though I am lost without you
As if I could search the world through and through.
This captive feeling would attack
And bring me back to you.

The past is gone
The pain is a song.
And I sit alone
Collecting tears from my cheek,
Tears that display
The mess that is me.

Dance in my mind like a slow motion picture
Wave your arms as the charming victor.
Leave you now – as swiftly as you came,
Leave you now – this beautiful family, this name.

Perhaps, I am a man too poor for your kind
A man too poor to purchase more of your time.

I stumble to find what is real anymore,
Tonight your ghost walks these halls

And crosses this floor
Just as she has a thousand times before.
I murmur, *Be Still*
At the sight of your apparition.
She vanishes for a moment
Taking with her perdition –
Only to return as I am fast asleep.
Starved, I see you in my dreams
Preying upon my lonely soul –
You still try to keep.

I awake clutching my heart,
Bleeding like the sifting sands
Through the hourglass.
These tired eyes search
tear-stained sheets for your cold hand.

A few days from now
Until I am rendered completely incomplete.
Two souls walk separately.
My soul, my heart – doth bleed
My body in weakened state shakes.
My heart, my soul – doth weep.

You have won,

There is nothing left to take

As these tears flood 'round my broken feet.

[07 december 2005. another panic attack — awoke
on the floor at 4 a.m. — last days at "home."]

winter of diffidence

sipping warmth from a mug
a memory of winter's magic
the crisp healing air
inhaled without care
thinking less of what's tragic.

as desire burns to ash
a tattered life inherits reality
come this winter i'll be one
two having come undone
summer having stripped morality.

o take me back to the snow
lost in a land of white
a look from her eye
in the sweet by and by
embraced by fire's light.

shaken awake again by a dream
as organs beat like symphony

the stars have all hid
happiness under lid
a deadly winter has come for me.

the calendar turns rapidly
to a favored time of year
warmth under blanket
comfort as we make it
now in death grows as fear.

do tell, shall i shallowly grasp
whatever woman will have me
holding tightly through
these months so cold and few
till dead leaves turn to green.

o how doth this belittled heart leave
a bloodied past behind
a past as old as yesterday
needing colour to paint away
the pain that aims to script and to define.

[09 october 2005. 11:58 p.m. –
what kind of man will I now be?]

blind

i'm thumbing through the memories
searching for the words
dreaming in black and white
but living shades of grey
i'm picking up the pieces
from the corners of the earth
ones laced with intentions
of leaving you behind.

[10 october 2005. the night of our anniversary –
she's vanished and nothing seems real.]

bewildered and punchdrunk

i had a
hopeless dream
that smiled
from the depths
of me.
it was just
a tiny seed –
one i
did not
water
nor feed.

time passed
and
seasons changed.
suddenly,
this small seed
had a name –
and small
it was
no longer

as it
enveloped all
of me.

for the soil
was so pure
that its roots
wrapped 'round
my soul.
beautiful vines
tightly tied
'round a
beating heart
of gold
setting love
free
to search
like a lost
foal.

in an instant
love landed
as stars
aligned

through the windows
of the sky.

my gaze fell
deep into her
eyes
and i drank the
wine.

for months
i staggered
drunk
from one
moonless night.
finding not a
remedy
to ease a troubled
mind.

alas
i seemingly
stepped away
but it has
followed.

leaving only
time
in its wake.

how
can one tell
a
hopeless
dream
that nobody
wants you
when you're
alive?

it is a question
without an
answer —
one a beating
heart
still tries
to find.

these strange days

i let you in
close enough
to watch me sleep

and you left a hole in me

i let you dance
close enough
for skin to blend

and you left a hole in me

i let you look
close enough
to see the love i hide

and now i watch the smoke rise
from where you left a hole in me.

ghost ship

how do i explain over the edge
to a world that is round.

how am i still heard
when i no longer make a sound.

take away the pictures
leave no memories in the clouds.

purge all i've done
find not grace that doth abound.

fill me up – pour me out
till i'm six feet under ground.

all i am is a cargo hold
and a will that has (finally)
allowed.

status quo

the future has sold out

someone has compromised the end

abort the mission

call off the launch

there's no use in attempt

to figure this trend.

all hands on deck

now it's back to bed

let the truth be told

as time i've grown cold

wasting away

a soul

half living

half dead.

hiding the hyde

imitate to create
a better man than me.

smile mixed with frown
gloating when i'm down
just to hear me bleed.
a glimpse into the mirror
staring down the fear
meeting a face so sinister
a face that does agree.

is there anything left
of the man in the sea
has he gone and died
or is he – now me.

awake

wake up
just to stare at the wall

the heaviest thoughts
make their way to the front

it's like a thousand words
weigh a thousand pounds

and a knock on the door
will push me further in.

putting a knife to all ties
makes it easier to defend

as the sun goes down
and the lights go out

i sleep just to
do this
all over again.

favored dimension

i long for
the night
as i long
for dreams.
for in the
night it can
appear a dream.
and in dreams
one can get
plenty of sun,
see the
colours of
the day
and live years
on end
without sleep.
in both
night and
dream you
must wake
from sleep.

and when you do
the night
is gone
and the dream
is gone.
and you are
left with
an entire day
of longing
for night
and longing
for dreams.

with scrapbook and tape

the pictures
the pictures
they are never good
for me. I get lost
going from one
to the
next.

to the next.

the pictures
they hide the things
best kept as such.
they perfect the
things that are not
as such. they
take me to places
i ought not go
dreaming of a
white picket fairy
tale.

the pictures
they are not good
for me.

i dream a thousand
words before i
sleep.
and when i let
go and sink into
the deep
she is right
there with me.
and that deadly
imagination fills the
blanks between the
frames and make her
out to be much more
than she ought. and
when
i come to in the
morning light
she
should look differently.

but
she doesn't
she's the same as in
the pictures and
the frames
in
between.

Walk Away

I came alone
I left with her.
She left me
I came with you.
You left me
And played with them.
I sit here
A fool again.

(Lesson.)
Better alone
Than in Eve's hand.

Phoenix

Things are changing
Ever changing
Always turning
Always growing.
They are pruning
I am glowing
They are preening
I am gleaning.

Then they started a fire
And I burnt to ashes.

602

Fuck you
for telling
me my
heart was
black and dark
ugly and marred.

Fuck you
for using
his name
to proclaim
that I must
be renewed
from shame.

Fuck you
for coddling
with coo
the lies
fed to you
with fork

and with
spoon.

Thank you
for all you
believed
which
gave me
the keys
to set myself
free.

Churched

You left me
I know you did
I called your name
And you
Were not there
You lied to me
You
Defiled me
Sat me up straight
And eyed me
You cried to me
Altar and confide in me
You said you hung
And died for me
You played the part
Appeased the heart
Waving branches
For all to see

Yet I was not there
And neither was He.

speakeasy

i was once a frail man.
thin skin
weak hands.
but not anymore.

i was once an open book.
unguarded
have a look.
but not anymore.

i once let everyone in.
all smiles
all kin.
but not anymore.

earn your stay.
is how i must play.
both now,
and ever more.

I Came Upon

Yet another Christmas
Spent completely alone
Realizing
I was nothing
Without family
Without home.

I ceased to exist
On a midnight clear
I was like
The fell foliage
In the covered wood
Which none could
Hear.

méchante femme

everything here is old
reminding me of you.
it's time to move on
move on to something new.

something a little more me
and a lot less the fool.

At the Sight of Defeat

PART I

Stipple on my skin
The names you say within
And I'll walk around with them.
Press into my brain
All the days of shame
And I'll topple from the weight.
Bury all of me
In the belly of the beast
And I'll go quietly.

PART II

I'll wait patiently.

———————————————————————

I'll rise and hover over the Earth.
I'll take to the wings and blot out the Sun.
I'll bathe in the blue and unlock the Middle.
And you won't soon forget
The memory of me.

LOVE
AND
EVERYTHING
BELOW IT

Snow Before Melt

You can't say Love
is messy.
You can say mankind
is messy.
You can say life
is messy.
But not Love.
Love is pure,
And if anything
But Love
Is coupled with Love –
Love ceases to exist.
For Love
in any season
Can only be
Love.

A Journey to the Water's Edge

A heavy fog
lay across
the harbor.

The beacon
atop the
lighthouse
made its way
through
to all
the ships at sea.

The silence
was broken
by the cry
of a lonely
gull.

As I reached
the cliff
the roaring
of the waves

crashing
upon the rocks
drowned out
the gull's cry.

I sat on
the edge
and studied
the ocean's front
each wave
born to
magnificently
die.

I spotted
the gull
riding the
wind above me
as a kite
tethered
to the ground.

Yet he was
slave to

no one —
he was as free
as the
leaves of
autumn.

Free to rise
and fall.
Free to cry
and
free to call.

I pulled my
pen and paper
out from
my satchel
and began
to write
a letter
to my
elusive Love.

Whispering
each word

to the sky
as I wrote.

For if God
would not
bring her
to me —
perhaps fate
would answer
my cry,
my gull's call.

The wind
grew more
severe as
I finished
my prose
and
emblazoned
my name
across the
bottom.

The sea
rose in
intensity
as if it
were eagerly
anticipating
my proclamation.
Like a young pup
head chasing tail
waiting for
the ball
to be thrown.

I rose
to my feet
as I spun
the letter
into a circle
and slid it
into the
belly of
the bottle.

Shoving
the cork
to seal
with all
my might,
I took a
few steps
away from
the cliffs edge.

Pausing
for a moment
I tilted
my head
towards the sky.

As I
let out a sigh
I brought
the bottle
to my lips

kissed

its neck

for safekeeping

and let it fly.

the time-traveler's life

the sting
of it all
is how each
one breathes.
she seemingly
never misses a beat
as he
holds his
breath
until their eyes
can again
sync.

his world
is on pause.

as she
is the cog
that makes time
spin on
its axis,
that tells him

he

is not

alone.

that his energy

has a

partner –

a

soul cut

from

neighboring clay.

he fears

that her

soul

of wanderlust

will never be

free –

he fears

it will hold fast

and remain

under key.

lost for all

of this life.

his lungs may
burst
and carry him
home
as they hold
his breath,
even still,
in hopes that
she
will be
ready
for he
in the next life.

and in his
demise
he will pay
a hefty price.

stop on red, leave on green

tonight
i saw you again
crossing
the same
street in
the Village.

you remind me
of the girl
i fancy –
the one with
the sleeve
of tattoos,
yet thinner
and a bit
less gypsy.

still
Bohemian –

yet,
stirred
with an aura
of class
elegance, really.

this time
i ghosted myself
next to you
on the white
line
of the
crosswalk,
as the
digital bird
sang to the
blind.

i walked
by your side
to see
where you
went after
crossing that

same street
day on end
as the sun
dove below
the merchants
casting shadows
on each passer by.

will you
slip into the
used bookstore,
past the rows
of fiction
and biography
to clasp hands
on poetry
and read –
under breath
wishing
flowery words
were written
for thee?

will you
stop in the
busy
coffee dive
and substitute
for tea
with two cubes
of sugar
and a dash
of cream?

will you
bounce your
knee
and anticipate
a man who
has spoken
for thee –
or do you sit
alone to
drink in
the warmth

and dream,
dream,
dream ...

with haste
you wisp
away
into a smoky
haze
as
the car behind
sounds its
single note
revelry
causing me
to look up
and see
that i had
failed to notice
the light
turn to
green.

the wolves have eaten you

soft haired girl
wide-eyed with wonderment
sleeping heart of good intent
so eager for something new
dining with the elders
drinking in the wine
mixed with wisdom
sinking in the cushions
listening to the sensuality
of French tongues
under flickering candle light
slipping out into the dark cold wind
leaving three decades to slumber
while you hide under heavy books
twirling a diamond circle
waiting for your decision
to fall among the wolves.

Under Fruitless Moon With Watery Eye
(The Lunatic, the Lover and the Poet)

I am in love with thine own fiction

I create the impossible and wish it to be

Letting it sink only so deep

A mixture of Shakespeare and symphony

At this hour, I love but a voice

Singing me to sleep

Which is where I can dream

As flowers of magic brush eyelids under tree

It is there where the siren doth follow me

Ah, but in this dream

My fiction is reality

Her soft skin I can touch

The voice I can feel

As she sings – head at rest

Safely upon my chest

It is here I can run fingers

Through crimson hair

It is here where the stranger

Is stranger no more

Wake me not, oh cruel world

Oh staunch bland reality

Reality that finds delight in leaving me empty

Arms void of she – or anybody

Leave me here in a Midsummer Night's Dream

Where love is more than a theme

Where Love is my living breathing entity

Where she is everything

And I, I am her revelry

Her gallant knight on warrior steed

It is here where I allow myself to be loved

To seek need

To find all these things in her unending reprieve

A haven from reality's sting

The cold cruel vice of distant memory

Where love was a game

A fairy toy

An antique fabled plaything

Where every demon was after thee

The victor those who made me bleed

Points awarded for suffering

Nay reality, steal not this fine enchanting

Oh siren keep to singing

Hold me tighter

Perchance, take me deeper in dream

Into this wide open scene

Vivid fields with blooming seed

Colour aglow on blankets of green

Into the forest of plenty

Oh set me free

Take all of this need, release and appease

Replace with eyes of longing glean

Eruption of creativity

Gift to me

Love – passion – your utmost being

Save me from euphoric imagining

Save me from this fine frenzy.

West Eighty-first

Where from I write
Perched with pen
I see the city
I take her in

The lovers they lie
In grasses of green
The streets they sing
Songs wind doth bring

Painted in serenity
Held with calming breath
Awaiting my turn
To unravel this mess

Make sense of this
I do solemnly plead
Rid doubt and birth
Love that will bleed.

battle ready

i am rather taken
by the mystery
of you
yet, with each
word
that unravels
the illusion
i sink deeper

i long for more

my heart
takes to wings
inside it's chamber
longing to be
loosed
longing for
but a glimpse
of this creature
that is you.

i find my mind

at ease

no longer crafting fiction

to appease

no longer

standing guard

at every entry

every port at sea

be it intrigue

be it the ever present

need to see

or be it

the lust to find

a dust born angel

to journey

along side thee.

moon and stars

be damned

if they do not

hold the light

of the sun

long enough

for me to reach you.

oceans be cursed

if their waters

wall up the way

to your heart

and crash upon

my body

filling my lungs

with the weight

of a thousand

screams.

and if the

mountains

rise and fall

in line

as an army

of suitors

lying in wait

hiding in shadows

scheming to steal

your heart

i would

rise above

and put them
under my heel
one step
at a time
and with each climb
i would
conquer another
leaving it silent
as it sinks
back into the earth.

sing sweetly to me
siren of safety
guide me with
a soft voice
that reaches
the depths of me
for my ear
stands ready
listening
in each breeze
sent by western winds
longing to hear
gentle words

that will lead me

to lie

beside quiet waters

that will quench my desire

to bathe in

something so real

that death

could not cut it

from my soul.

jet black hair

your embrace
as we parted
at the end
of the drive
was deliberate
and intoxicating
you held tightly
and i let go
far too soon.

with needle & thread

she's like the thread woven through
the quilt of my life
maybe she is holding me together
or maybe i'm extra lonely tonight
i can't let go of those fireworks in the sky
the ones i saw when i closed my eyes
as she pressed her lips to mine

a first kiss can be like a drug
a cancer on the inside of your mind
i was freshly 19 in the back of a friend's van
on the way home from a hockey game
when she decided to alter my course
i don't think she realized just what she'd done –
she fused us together when she took the first one

i loved like only a newborn could
and the world was mine for the conquering
she loved with reckless abandon
like nothing could ever die
we were sharing young lovers lips at every given chance
twice caught by police in city parks after dark

and on the family couch where parents checked hands –
something only seen in the films of the 50's
something only funny when the flashing lights
and God-fearing parents left
left us kissing again and again

and in the summer months of '96
she sewed together the first patch
with needle and with thread.

the year oasis owned my discman

i met
you
when you
were
with him
you rode
along
to the
little
coffee shop
shows
he and i
would play
until
one day
you broke
it off

the following
Sunday
you and i

sat next
to each other
at the
evening service

during the
standing
and the singing
you reached
over and
took my
hand
fingers –
interlocking

the world
stopped
spinning
you looked
me
in the eyes
and gave
me

a smile
from the side
that i can
still see
sixteen years
into the future

you left
early
and we
never spoke
a word of it
and i
never
saw you
again

in my
sleeping dream
i still
see you
at
eighteen
walking away

i can't even

remember your

name

yet when

Wonderwall

plays

or your

scent

comes

my way

i can

see that

smile from

the side

perchance

one day

i'll be

walking down

the street

and you'll

come up

beside

take my

hand
fingers —
interlocking
and the
world will
once again
stop
spinning.

eyes like heaven

as we lay
skin entwined
i wished
every day
would end
with this
night.

almond shaped
windows
painted with
sepia tones
catching light
from a
slow drifting
moon.

neither spoke
as memories of old
provoked
the unwinding
hope

which would come
to be
this night.

adolescent butterflies
danced about
the room
and landed upon
the insides
as the sun would
soon rise
and define
the imprint
in the skies
of us,
this night
and our separate
lives.

The Edge of Love

Here it comes again
A smile could bring my end.
Progress not to anything more
A friendship forever is better, adored.
Hold me now the whole night through
Stopping there creates need for you.
Trust placed in human comfort
Sutures the wound – reveals the hurt.
Handle with care
I whisper, "beware."
Release now the thought
Of love in the time of Camelot.

november letters

i sit tonight with chardonnay by candlelight
a pile of letters at my side
pondering thoughts that i must write
as i listen under your sky
and read the words that i denied
on your cold november night.

it would kill me if we said goodbye
is it too late now to make it right
missing you three years out of sight
could you have saved me from this plight.

let me now walk the ocean floor
proving you deserve more
more than a dance on our Malibu shore
a longing glimpse of fate to adore.

pursue me now as you wanted to then
hearing your voice – whispers in my head
this heart sewn out on sleeve again
your strength and hope for all time
there for you morning and night.

it's my turn now to put up a fight
needing a shoulder for which to cry
a soul disassembled barely alive
leave Rome now and rebuild my life.

a cup of mystery overflows
not a word spoken or glimpse from the grove
stuck in a moment waiting to unfold
a future of happiness and peace untold.

o love now would you be so bold
rescue me from this blistering cold
restore me
cure this dire need
of you – endlessly.

little red book

i'm writing
this morning
in the little
red book
you gave me.
the one you
bought while
in Italy.
i remember
it matched
your lips
and flushed
cheeks.

hours of
love
had passed
skin on
skin.
in the morning
glow

in the after-
glow.
you rolled
over
kissed
my nose
and said –
i have
something
for you.
it was sweet
you were
sweet.

i haven't
seen you
since
we met
for dinner
and
drinks
at our
place
on the

corner

in Germantown.

where you

asked

that i return

your

poetry books.

i had them

in my car

and that

may

have ruined

everything –

at least

your

temporary

fancy free

fling.

it's been

a handful

of months

and i think

i miss you

or perhaps
it's just that
last night
i watched
Marilyn
perform
on the silver
screen
and made
the connection
that you
share the
same face —
that open
lipped
gaze.
that soft-skin
that
i praised.
or maybe
it's just
because
i picked
up

this
little
red book
that
you gave.

A Saturday on Broadway

There's the one
With the legs
And the rainboots
That I felt near
That I saw across
The way.
I was with
The one that
Was helping me
Let go.
We were all
There
And warhol
Was trying to
Convince us
That he
Ever made
Anything worth
A shit.
Both the legs
And the eyes

Believed him
With wool
At the ready.

But I couldn't
Believe.

cleaning house

today while
sorting through
my library of books
a piece of paper
fell from the
pages of one
titled
The Sacred Romance
one i hadn't opened
in years

on the paper
was scribbled
a name
a phone number
and a location
the name
the phone number –
the ex
the location –
Desert Ridge,

in front of the
outdoor fireplace
it was the first time
i called her
the first time
we'd met
that fated day
in january
of two-thousand three

here I sit
eight years later
holding that piece of paper
wanting to call back
the number
and when she'd answer
i'd say,

i don't think it's a good idea
that we go on this date
i've seen our future
you're a horrible person
and i'd like to cancel,
i hope you understand.

[Pain]tings

Today I sold
The paintings
Inspired by your
Rejection.

A thousand dollars
Momentarily
In my pocket,
Yet the memories
And sting remain.

love and loss under irish skies

many detours
held this
morning's road
to you.

caffeine
heightens my
nerves
as i now sit
in the woods
by the river
and wait for you.

my mind is
so consumed
by the dust
of us
that it fails
to tell my lungs
to breathe.

i know that
it is over.

you know
that it
is over.

yet here
we are
to say it
out loud.

pour the
poison
into my
ears.

let it trickle
down my
throat.

let me
look upon
you once

more
before
my eyes
close
the windows
to my soul.

there
it is.

the stench
of the death
of Love.

i turn
and walk
away.
with each
parting step
comes the
pouring rain.

rain that
won't wash
this
painful stain,
rain that
won't hide
these crying
eyes.

rain that
brings
love
and loss
under
Irish skies.

The Stairwell

The door
opens to the
stairs
where
I let you in
before.
Forbidden
yes
yet
we both
wanted more.

The second hand
broke
the moment
neither spoke
on the fourth
where
I shed
the last
watery hope.

I held
your shoulders
against
my chest
and when
I let go
Love left
and we lost
its hold.

As my body
went stiff
I recounted
each moment
asking why
then
what if.

Weeks passed
and as
atrophy
surrendered
its grasp

eyes could
no longer
look their
last.
I pulled
myself
out of
the water
with a great
splash
and an
even
greater gasp.

Holding my
breath
again
I
descended
the stairwell
and
closed
the door
so that

you
were never
let
back in.

Already Strangers

Remember
when we first met?

You let me share
a table
with you
in the Village.
I had on
headphones
read a
poetry book
kept to myself.
You had on
that purple
scarf
that twinkle
in your eye
and
kept to the
questions.

I thought it
was funny how
after answering
I would
put my
headphones
back on
but before
I could press
play
another question
came dancing
my way.

Soon enough
you left
and I didn't
ask for
a way to
keep in touch
Better to let
the stars decide,
I thought.

Two months
passed
and I saw
you again.
We took to
the same spot
I had the
same drink
and a
different book.
You had
that same
smile and
different questions.
This time
I left the
headphones off
and started to
let you in.

Soon enough
we were
watching the
sun set

at Radnor,
taking walks
in my
neighborhood
and sharing
movies at
the Observatory.

You told me
you were
sick
and I was
worried.
Some days
you played
like it was
a walk in the park
other days
I thought
surely you
were dying.
You told me
to let the
world see

your journals
if the Black
Lung took you
away.
I told you to
burn mine if
a car crash
took me
away.

In the mornings
I worked on
my book
at your
kitchen table
while you
went to the
hospital
for more
needles
and more
horrendous
treatments.

When you
returned
I'd make eggs
and coffee
for breakfast
and we'd
lie on the
floor and
listen to
the music.

When the
moon would rise
we'd take
to cold sheets
and make
them warm.
Fitting together
like two
pieces of a puzzle.
We'd make
love
like the
Christians do.

With our
undergarments
on.
Always on.
We'd talk about
the chemistry
between us.
Always about
the chemistry.

Then one
night you
said you were
afraid of me.
Lacking
description,
you sounded
 like her.
And I had to leave.
I couldn't
explain myself
and neither
could you.

Time passed
until you
showed up at
my doorstep
to say that's
not
what you meant.
And we went
back to making
cold sheets
warm.

Lying there
you said you
couldn't imagine
me
not in
your life.
And that
God
crossed our paths.
That perfect
Christian line.
Always a line.

That night
you left with
a sparkle
in your eye
and that
charming smile.
Always that smile.

Time passed
and I called you.
No answer.
No ring back.
More time passed.
Text messages
were sent.
No texts back.

The roulette
wheel spun
as I tried to
understand.
Like understanding
how the sun
hung in the sky,

how the
baby bird
flies.
Or how
the moon
rules the
rising tide.

A month
passed
and I saw
you again.
You were at
Baja
dining with
a friend.
You hurried
to discard
your tray
acting fully
engaged
so as to
lead me to
think

you just
didn't see.

The only way
out was
directly to
my left,
the side
where you
used to lie.
You took
to the exit
with prestige,
turning your
head away
to hide as
you slid by,
holding your
breath and
squinting your
eye.

With a voice
just above a
whisper
I turned
and replied,
Don't worry,
we're already
strangers.
Only cold sheets
tonight.

dream up the world you want
and you'll be alright

while working
well into the
morning hours
Zooropa
started screaming
from my speakers –
i stopped
everything
and was transported
to the park
where we sat
in her yellow Jeep
as the sky
spun 'round
us that night.

i needed to
be back
there, engulfed
by the newness

sharing passion
for sound –
drinking in her
young eyes
of wait
and want.

but i
couldn't
then –
and i surely
can't now.

the singer
complies
and in this time
it's my
lonely demise.
for i have
no
compass
i have no map

i have no

reasons —

no reasons

to

get

back.

the touring syndrome

i miss taking pictures
with girls
holding one close
placing cheek against
cheek
soft smooth skin
capturing sweet scents
smiles on faces
memories
and history traces
hands on waist
touch – embrace
and that simple satisfaction
of filling a need
oh how i miss taking pictures
with girls.

it's nothing you wouldn't do

i saw her again
today.
which is nothing
out of the ordinary.
if i go there
she is usually
there. always quick
to give me a smile
attached to eyes that
gaze just a bit longer
than average. a bit
longer than someone
should gaze at a regular
ordering a cup of coffee.
she looks as if she's
searching for a clue
or an answer. or
waiting to give an
answer. i sit
down, open
my laptop and
set off to get

a bit of writing
done. i notice
her. she
hesitates
to notice me.
albeit she
was the one
who first
approached
asking what i
did. wanting details
making me
take notice.

an hour passes
my phone rings
i answer it and
talk for about
ten minutes. while
i'm on the call
i lock eyes with her
from across the room.
forget what i'm saying –
she gives me another

smile. this time there
is no question that
she wants to know more
she sees a future. i
smile back. i see
a future. how lengthy
a future –
at least 5 minutes
and a cup of coffee.
i let the moment leave
as i always do. with her
i always do. i think –
next time the moment
arrives i'll take it.
i'll whisper a phrase
set wheels into motion
and i'll say those simple words.
words i haven't been able
to say in years. i excuse
their use with fears of
rejected silence.
and let another day pass.

there's always a moment
and always a counter-
moment. one that
makes me think she's not
interested.

maybe she thinks
i'm just a weirdo with
long hair that is
interesting to look at.
maybe she thinks i should
join a traveling circus
show. the freak
show. the bearded lady,
the two-headed man
and me. come one!
come all!
sit and stare at
this boy!
try if you may
but you'll never
understand!
what a wonder -
what a marvel!

i end the
call and she's
gone.
either on her
lunch break or
the end of
her shift. i go back
to my writing.
i can always go
back to
my writing. it
never rejects –
it looks at me fearfully
and wonders if
i will abandon it.
but i won't. it's too
easy. it's cheating the
noise. a free pass
to sanity. an
excuse to live.

i leave for an
appointment with my
psychoanalyst.

i return an hour
later to have another
coffee and coddle
with my writing. i don't
tell the psychoanalyst
about her. i am fraught
that the psychoanalyst
will think i should join
a traveling circus
show. the freak
show.

i don't share her
with anyone.

this time she is
sitting at the bar-
top where i was
an hour before.
i leaned against the
counter and waited for
my coffee.
i asked her what
she was reading —

she answers
and i don't know
how to respond because
i think it's a shit read
i think the author
is a one-trick pony.
a snake oil peddler.
so i don't say much
other than to
tell her i had read
it. i wanted to be
honest. but honesty
would kill
anything living.
even though there was
nothing living. i asked if
she had finished with
work for the day, hoping
that would lead to
an asking of her to
accompany me
to dinner

but she
responded with,
 i am finished
but about to
leave — i just want to
read these last
five pages.

i didn't even
respond. i just stood there
and waited for
my coffee.
before it was placed
on the counter i
snatched it, mumbled
thanks and walked
away
straight to the corner
where i opened my
laptop and
set off to get
a bit of writing
done.

an hour later i
looked up and she
was gone
leaving me to return
tomorrow, order a coffee
and go back to
my writing.

she [la scène d'ouverture]

tonight i saw her
again
i walked past her sitting quietly eating her gelato
listening to friends of the indie scene converse
i was alone
as most nights these days.

i wandered into the video store
searching aisles for something to inspire
i daydreamed of what she would want to watch
what would she choose?

i collected my thoughts enough to decide
at the checkout i was hardly coherent
just nodding to whatever the teenager said
still thinking of her,

perhaps i'll say something on the way out
then again
thoughts of knowing never turn out better than not.

the bell on the door let out a jingle
she didn't look up
i nervously walked by
studying her intriguing face
"look up"
i said to myself as i approached her.

i muttered for chance
"grant me a look in the eye"
a small yet satisfying token to live on –

there was nothing.

she let me pass her by as a cool breeze
on a hot summer night.

i left her unaware
never knowing how i felt
and she left me fully aware
that i am still just a small shy boy
fearful of being shot down
afraid to take a chance.

she [le deuxième acte]

i walked up the stairs
there she stood
cute as a button
enchanting as the wood

a thousand words
leapt from mine eyes
not one landed
as i held in a sigh.

i took her hand
but only for a moment
wishing time i could stop
as i searched for atonement,

she was swept away
with the haste hence she came
a chance with fair Capulet
left nary mark spark nor flame.

the night took its time
wings strapped by its side

heart palpitating
too swift to divide

i slid near the wall
with ghostly intent
i felt her draw near
as i bathed in lament

i turned, thoughts of speaking
she was thus occupied
transpose of glance
another chance, passing by.

leaving music behind
i faded out
into the rain
visions of she
remain
brushed
in mantle frame.

thought persuades dream [she – acte de clôture]

as my mind pulled focus from blurry to sharp
she was standing beside me, almost, in the dark

a film to the right flickered on display
an emotional scene, overwhelming, portrayed
we slid inward together – our shoulders did touch
i crossed my arms, giving her hand a slight brush

leaving contact i awaited an unknown surprise
she slid her soft hand underneath mine
words fail to describe what followed after
the warmth of connection – life void of disaster

one by one all of our days played out
scene by scene i was never in doubt
we were inseparably together from touch till the end
with the film reel sputter lids blink to open

as my eyes pulled focus from blurry to sharp
i realized i was alone, almost, in the dark.

putting on sheets

i just put fresh sheets
on the bed
and
it made me miss
those times the ex
and i used to
make our bed together
not that I can
really remember
a particular time
this actually did happen.

maybe it's just that i
wish i had someone new
to put the other side on
and
climb in with
i hate walking around to
the other side
sometimes i just leave it be
as it still haunts me —

certain moments in life
remain frozen in time.

it's like having a handful of watches
and when the battery dies in one
time stops right then and there
and
if no one comes along to replace
the battery in that dead watch
the last time that watch worked
is the last moment it remembers
and
if you look at that watch
you are taken right back
to where it ticked its last.

these days i have a lot of
dead watches
combined with fresh sheets
and a bed half made.

Spectacle

You float across the room
With your smile and your charm
Your glance seems so shy
As if you sense harm
Avoidance breeds curiosity
Silence sounds the alarm
Speak so that it be known
You're more than visions from afar
Be a voice of intellect
Paint a universe of stars
Beckon truth and life
Come now raise the bar
Mystery loves company
Minds to maim and mar
Specks of colour leave your eyes
Curiosity left in shards
Confusion breeds discontent
As now time has erased smile and charm.

cicada

she's in Chicago tonight
or somewhere else
up north.

i don't ask
because i don't want to
miss her.

oh i'm allowed to
miss her
it's not that.

it's just that
if i decide to
miss her
i start to let myself
become attached.

and that is
where the allowing
and not allowing
comes into play.

so i decide
to sit in my
current state of limbo
where she has lifted
the rug to sweep me
under
but suddenly walked away.

leaving the rug
disheveled
and me
lying on the
floor in a pile.

The Other Side of Me

I'm not easy to love
Nor easy to please
Look through the mirror
To the other side of me.
Let go of what you want
What you think you need
Step into the glass
To the other side of me.
Feel around inside
Step lightly where I bleed
Wipe away the smoke
See the other side of me.
Drink in the passion
Off my life do feed
Binge off this dying person
You are the other side of me.

W

O where has the fun of chase fled?
Have I grown old with childishness,
Awaiting *the* night of wed?
Bright eyed full of wonder
O when will it cease,
This wishing well feeling
That does no better than to increase.

pirates by day, lovers by night

last night
before bed
i tucked myself
in and read
about pirates
and magnificent
battles
at sea.

yet when
i drifted off
i dreamt
of you and me
in the kitchen
where
we were
preparing dinner
and drinks.

i slid
my arm around
your waist

and
pulled you close
to my side.

as i kissed
the crown
of your head
i whispered,

*i can't believe
it's really you*

i must have
rolled over
as
all of a sudden
we were
in a field
lying on our
backs and
watching the sky
turn shades of blue.

suddenly

the largest

raven i had

ever seen

took to the trees

and called out

to me.

magically

with comfort

and ease

you turned

to me

with that

gaze of

longing and

leaned in

to

press your

lips to mine

and

just as my

lips touched

yours

we were
interrupted by
the booming sound
of my neighbor
slamming shut
the garbage lid
just outside
my bedroom
window.

i begged you
not to go
as i fought
back
a rousing
consciousness
but it was
too late.

you faded
up and
away
into wisps
of dancing

smoke
like the
final ember
of a candle
after dying
in the wind.

i cracked
open
my sand-
filled eyes
to see
if you were
lying
next to me
but all
my focus
gave
was the book
of pirates
and
magnificent
battles at sea.

Birds of a Feather

Kiss the wind

Do it again

Feel the breeze

Careless

Carefree

Take flight

High

As a kite

Let go

Oceans throw

Swim

Spin

Do it again

Together now

Let's kiss the wind.

leaving the muse at home

i stopped by
her place
at a quarter
after one
in the morning.
i was tired,
beyond tired –
but i had to see
her.
she embraced me
at the car
and asked that i
come up.
i declined –
the sounds
of party-goers
emanated
from the patio.
crowded rooms
give me that
tight collar
feeling.

i noticed she
was cold
so we sat
in the car,
hiding from
the wind.
i kept looking
at her
and smiling,
awkwardly –
i don't think
i own a smile
that doesn't feel
awkward as
it leaves.

those eyes,
that face –
sealed with lips
like sugar.
she kept looking
at me
and smiling,

showing that
adorable twist.

Vanessa Paradis
was exhaling
softly from the car
permeating the
night air –
laughing
she said,
i hate this!
don't you have
any Ramones?
while sipping
on a Miller
Lite.

she's not like
the muse
in my head,
quite the
contrary.

i suppose
that's the intrigue –
that, and
she's an
actual person.

time sped up
and
slowed
down
for the next
thirty minutes
as we
played
with each
other's hands
while looking
out over
the lake.
i wish the fountain
lights were on
for you,
she said.

and when
she did
i felt my
heart
glow from
inside its
cage.
she displayed
that
she paid
attention,
gets what
gets me.

the night was
drifting away
from us
and i had
to leave.
i asked her
if we could
spend the
following
evening together.

of course!
she said
leaning in,
laying soft
lips to
mine —
lips like
sugar.

the revolving door just outside my heart

i was tucked in the corner
breathing exceptionally well
i had finished my oatmeal
and was waist deep in
Bukowski's
The People Look Like Flowers
At Last
i read and read
until my coffee
went cold.

i looked up from
my book
in time to see
the girl i was
spending my evenings
with
fly by –
her bright red
heels
interrupting the
hardwood floor,

click-clock
click.
i'm not the kind
to flag her down
or call out her name –
besides,
she was in my arms
just last night
and will probably
repeat tonight.

a few verses later
i received a text message
from the New York
fashion queen
the one that asked of me
to take her virginity
earlier this year.
she said that
i was the perfect man
to teach her
followed by
the perfect man to wed her.

in today's text message
she asked if i had a
love life yet.
i responded,
i love life, for now
that's enough.
she replied,
i thought you were
dating that older woman
i laughed,
not at the prospect
but from where
it came.
i told her
that she had a great
imagination –
fueled by the
nonsense of the internet.

in a bizarre twist
of life is stranger
than fiction,
at that moment
the woman

we were texting about
walked up to me
and bent over to
squeeze my neck.
i set down my book
and phone
as she
began to unload
the pain behind
her eyes,
informing me
her boyfriend
just
broke up with her
via
email –
what a dog,
i told her.
i knew that
guy was
an asshole the
moment i met him.
continuing
i said,

all you can
do now is
let the pain
teach you.
i could have
recited the
alphabet
forward then
backwards –
it would have
had the
same effect.
she didn't
want words
she only wanted
human touch
i could see
it coming
off of her
like the
cold
emanating
from a
frozen highway.

fortunately,

i

am not

a

dog

who chases

every wagging

tail –

any animal

can devour

vulnerability.

she took her

sunglasses off

her head

and slid them

slowly

down

the fold

of her chest

and into her

tube top,

as if

i
didn't notice
prior to
this magic
trick.
my eyes
remained
trained
on hers —
like the good
Christian boy
i had been
raised to
be.

just then
my phone
alerted
everyone,
i had
a new
message.
i picked it
up to

see
that the
New York
fashion queen
had sent
me
a photo
of her smiling
in a cute
summer
dress
with the words
i'm waiting for you
tucked underneath.
i sighed as i lay
my phone
by my side
and
exchanged
a few choice
words
with the
heartbroken one
before she

left to be

alone

with her pain –

until she

could find

someone to

confide

with

human touch

and lay what bleeds

momentarily

to rest.

i went back

to my

cold coffee,

took a sip

and scribbled

these

lukewarm thoughts.

the artist

rum lips
with a red-
light kiss
waiting
to be finished
under
romantics in
Paris.

collecting a
new bag
of tricks
merging dreams
of sexual
things
with
the sweet
musings
reality brings.

awaiting both

at 11:59

on

New Years Eve,

2015.

entertain the angel

books and a guitar
strewn across my bed.

mind shots of an angel
bathing in my head.

a queen of sorts
a temptress of light.

words from the other side
guiding me this night.

her hands are distant
yet her body warm.

as if nothing existed
no qualms – no storm.

she breathes request to be near
when silence forms.

no thoughts of yesterday
just tonight and the morn.

come dawn we awake
apart yet more clear.

divine sent one more angel
to put asunder my fear.

Trip Wire

I formed in you
With ease and comfort
Safety held suspense
Freedom over hurt.

Eyes attached
Souls entwined
Mind halts healing
Church bred chime.

Come with me
Again and again
Stave my loneliness
Move my pen.

I can't sober up
No, not this time
Hold me close
Undefined.

I only want love

Not too much – just enough

Move with me

Oh rhythm – oh dove.

backward masking

young
childish
yet full of want
age of the studies
pen in hand
yet eyes on me
a glimpse
a smile
simple subtle tease
gritting your teeth
busting at the seams
more than a handful
of what i need
give me a night
alone
you
me
let me please
releasing the other
the darker side of me
throw away caution

let
lust
seethe.

eventually everything will be told

striped skirt
frilled white blouse
mustard yellow cardigan
keeping her close.

spinning a circle
on her hand
lips slightly open
showing a glint
of teeth.
she bites
the lower
and slides
her hand
up and down
the buttons on
her blouse.

she hides the circle
running her eyes
across the wood
grain of the table.

she ponders
she's lost in
a fabricated
world of want.

from the grain
she glances
up at him.
he feels her eyes
fall upon him –
the connection
is made.

in an unknown
dimension
all is surrendered
in a look
her eyes
fall back
to her book
as she touches
her hand
to her
lips

and releases
a hesitant sigh.
one of want
mixed
with her
present obligation.

she spins the circle
and stands up
from the table.
she gathers herself
and begins
to walk toward him
pausing
at his side
for
a single moment.

she holds her breath
closes her eyes
and walks
away.

Musing

That hair,
That blood red hair.
Setting those eyes apart,
Popping them forward
Like a 3D picture show.
That skin,
That milk-white skin.
Begging to be caressed
Hidden under
Strapless summer dress
Like a harvest moon
Veiled by soft drifting clouds.

Cloverleaf

On the corner
where lust
meets love
I dig a hole
and bury my head.

Allegorically Speaking

When I'm in
I want out
When I'm out
I want in
Let the breeding
Of confusion
Begin.

Wrapped In Black

I'm not

Like them

But I'm doing

What they

Do

So,

I try to

Relax

And ignore

The ugly décor

Rum and cloves

Beer and cigarettes

Mine, theirs

Ash remains

Blood thins

And I stay

Because she stays

And I long

To look again

One more look

To drink

Her in

One more
Look to
Breathe
Her again.

The Dark One

One by one
The options they fall
So simple to take
So easy to resolve

One for each night
With a cherry on top
Eat then repeat
So hard to stop.

Ebb/Flo

Colder than Boston
A night on the town
A vixen of sexuality
Lost in the sound
A night in her arms
Injected the poison
A pull of the hair
A bite from the chosen
Leaving her mark
Eyes caught by stare
Arrival beseech solitude
Sainted angels beware.

IV

It's Sunday
She wants in again.
I was okay with it
The first time
But now,
The second
Feels like sin.

torn little plastic parachute toy

have i ever
seen Love?
apart from a mother's –
is there such a thing?
it's always tried
to be tied
to this
and that.
do this
do that.
but if you won't
you're to be thrown
from a high-flying aero plane
without a parachute.

TINY
ARROWS
PIERCING
THE BLACK

Kinema

I am the great wanderer
I am like the wind
I can stay
Neither here
Nor there
I cannot be held
In – house
Or – box
For if the wind
Cannot roam
Cannot dance
Among the streets
Or in the stars
It will cease
To be.

bury the boy to save the man

one cannot become
his own man
lest he put the fearful child
that lives inside
to rest

we know why
he holds so tightly
to that frail
weeping boy

for it is in fact all that he knows
it is all he can see

the pain
that is real
has defined him

the scars
that remain
have shaped him

all that can be done
to save the man
is to put the boy to rest

for the boy
does not need to be held
or consoled
it is far too late for him
he can no longer feel comforting arms

we must remember him
we must
never
forget him
yet
we can no longer carry him

he has grown heavy
walking has become unbearable
the hills – too steep
the valleys – too wide
and time will not allow

for both
to make the journey

wear black to his wake
shed tears until your river
runs dry
hold his memory dear
know that he lived
and now dies
so the man
can have life

there is a reason
we leave the dead
to rest
there is a reason
we do not carry
their remains
the rest of the way

do not let
the lessons that he learned
be for naught
do not let his smile

escape your lips
do not let
the joy that he fought
so ferociously to hold fast
vanish
and do not let
the light that shone bright
in his eyes
leave yours

he is gone now
leave his body lie
rest weary arms
at your side
the dawn has begun
lift your weary head high
there is more weight to carry
now that this child has died

mourn you no more
leave tears dry
look now to the sky
and drink in the journey

for the boy

has saved my life.

little wooden memory box

as everything
i've known
floats above
and below
i take them
one by one
and define each
its own.

and when the
very last
has been filed away
i move forward
with my
drawer of treasures
that will never decay.

tiny arrows piercing the black

in a world
so inundated
and over-
saturated
with the LCD
flashing lights
and
monotonous
beeps
of technology
i find my
escape
in the darkness.

the subtlest
of light
and sound
can transform
my world
and take me
around

to another

place.

i speak of

this

as i sit

on a weathered

wooden deck

ten feet

above the

water's edge

on a remote island

in the Atlantic

where pirates

fought battles

and buried treasure

when the darkness

is now

as it was then.

the sounds they

surround me

the splashing waves

against
the docks
the icy rain
slamming into
wood and water
like tiny arrows
piercing
the black.

by the clockwork
of the seafaring
man
the beacon
from the lighthouse
shines an eerie
reflection
upon the choppy
waters
as if God
took a brush
of orange
and gold
and painted

upon the vast

expanse

of nothing

creating a moving

picture

slow and flickering

like the

ancient zoetrope

minute yet

complete.

you can

fake

and recreate

just about

anything

these days

but not this

moment.

this moment

is all mine.

clean your room before you go

i've thought about
a lot today.
the one i love
who doesn't say
it back,
the music
that moves me
from one room
to another
and the roaring
voice in my head –
that says, do you want
to vanish forever
unknown or
do you want the
future to know
your name.

what does an
artist work for
if it is not
to be remembered.

i find the
first response
to be
that i create
for myself.
to keep moving
forward,
to avoid tripping
in the weeds,
to keep from
going comatose –
to stave
creative atrophy.
yet below
the kick
i know this
to be an
untruth.
i do create
to move others.
even as this pen
moves across
this paper

somewhere in my
soul
i prey
it touches
another.

i find the loneliness
of poetry
to be a comfort.

line after
line.
words appear.
filling a once
empty
white room
with companions.

connecting –
dancing.
a breathing
organism of art.

i want to
leave that.

not so much
my name.

simply that.

and my love
for her
and
the music
that moves me
from one room
to another.

The Whisper of the Night

I am a vampire
Forced to live in daylight
Born among four wall dwellers
And proclaimers of selfish right.

In shadows I tried to remain
Walking among them for years
I listened as they laughed
I sat still as they jeered.

They knew not what I was
Trying every which way to kill
They know not what I am
Nor how, with blood, my valves fill.

On the corner of a roof
I have chosen to live
Denying feast of necks
Passing those who would give.

Skirts and sweet smells
Flourish to press will
Spinning webs to capture
Teasing with shapely thrills.

Drive away the demons
Drink the blood of grace
Growing weak in the eyes of man
I learn, I enjoy the taste.
Plot the ending of my art
Death the conventional way
Sunshine, stakes and silver
Rid not this man of clay.
Knowing I will outlive them all
Reveals a crooked smile
Collecting the corners of the earth
Every inch and every mile.
In wonder they have questioned
Appearing as still in prime
To most a distant memory
80 years past borrowed time.
I am a vampire
Forced to live in daylight
I have escaped the four wall dwellers
And I am the whisper of the night.

shortchanged

i dream at night of my ocean
whispering waves of forgiveness
depleting a journey i refuse to take
and a mistress of enchanting sands.

the shells of time refute me
the hour of disbandment draws nigh
the emotions lay dormant at the bottom
and my organs yield a response.

faltering in my youth
failing in my proclamations
longing for but a glimpse
of beauty and direction.

seeking after wisdom
only granted by the mysteries
of the ocean in which i dream
and the body in which i slumber.

[While performing the adulthood ritual of consolidating life's collected things I found this poem, shortchanged, amongst hundreds of other writings from my childhood – the year 1993 was written in the bottom left corner. It drastically stood out amongst the undeveloped sappy rhetoric, but more so holding it in my hand 20 years later sent chills through my being as I read these words penned by the 15 year-old me. It is nothing short of visionary, foretelling what lay ahead. It is as if the writer I have become today traveled back to share with that boy what was coming and gifted him the poet's mind to craft that one single piece.]

Inner Battle Royal

Scads of talentious elements
line the shelves inside my brain.
Maybe I am all of them.
Or, maybe.
I am the one I least want to be.
Alas, we dance in the ring.
Again.
And again.
And again.

never stop moving

if i were a metronome
i'd keep better time
everything would be done
with precision
left
then right
repeat.

make that knocking noise
so the world knows
you're working.

no breaking the rhythm
to stop and think
to question
to feel
run until it's unwound
and when it has
your time is up
the piano stops humming
and your song is over.

Ardent Fable

I am not who I claim to be
Yet rather
Who I aspire to see at the end of my week
I am not the man at the depths when I sink
Yet rather
The one who swam to the top of the drink
I am not the one who receives the acclaim
Yet rather
The one who toiled in the mud under rain
I am not the everyman's son you perceive
Yet rather
A child born to carry the flame
Beyond final fallen leaf.

The Searcher

I searched for the meaning of Life
Apart from the ways of youth
Where told what I know and what I see
Grew out from under each pew.

Tightly it wrapped
From ankle to waist
Then went the arms
Soon lips were erased.

A soldier in an army
Wooden, carved all the same
How high shall I jump?
As I surrender my name.

Cut out like a cancer
Never to grow back
Doors slamming shut
Upon stretch – by rack.

Left with books
Left with sound mind
Left to reconstruct
The meaning of Life.

Alone with idea
Alone with thought
Only one foe remained
Day and night I fought.

I cornered myself
Forcing final blow
I cut from the heart
I removed the circus show.

When the dust did settle
In pieces I remained
As blood stained the earth
I was half standing – half slain.

In the deafening silence
My name was called, thrice
Holding my dead I set West
Searching for the meaning of Life.

earth suit doctrine

i have left
the fold
to find true
peace
and sanctuary
in the solitude
of the
trees.

yes, the box
can be a comfort
a womb
of safety
so long as
you don't try
to think
outside
the parameters
of a
fabricated
modern
philosophy.

out here
it's the birds
who sing
praise
requiring not
smoke
lights
and camera
they don't
know what
craving
attention
means.
they have no
ego
to feed.

they merely
are
what they are —
and who
i am is who
i will
be.

i am just
a bird
of blackened
feather
flying through
the trees
observing everything –
occasionally
landing
to sing.

i hold no
affiliation
i wave no
flags of
proclamation
i learn all
that i can
from the first
drop of sand,
dissecting pages
and
conversing with sages.

the box will
say of me
that i am
backsliding,
running away
from God
a life hidden
from blessing.
some
will waste
hours on knee
praying for my
salvation
because they do
as they are taught
to do,
dismissing that each
has a need to
work out their
own.

worry not
for my soul.

every born
drop of blood
must find
what God is
and is not.

neither man
nor woman
can make
that decision
for another –
right and wrong
don't decide,
there is no
black and white
only separation
of darkness
and light.
of which both
serve a purpose
under the sun,
each as import
as the other.

life

is not linear

it is not

what happened

when

it is a sphere

a culmination

of the whole

no beginning

and no end.

i am

just a drop

of water

falling from

the heavens.

listen as i

make my way

down through

the

clouds,

watch me
as i mix
with the
ground.

but never
tell me
that you know
what i am
or what i
should be.
i am the
one who
has passed
through time
in this
earth suit
of skin –
and this
is my doctrine.

Raven Song

When I am lost
They caw for me
They call for me.
To show the way
To sing of peace.
They caw for me
They call for me.

The Boy in Me

"Play it again!"
The child pleaded.
"I must have it again!"
His patience retreated.

"It was the best yet,
And just what I needed."

"Play it again!"
The child repeated.

In Dreams

A mop for a crown
A blanket – the royal gown
Flying through the clouds
Above the maddening crowd
Alone and entirely me.

Awake in my bed
Monsters in my head
Closet on open hinge
Time to fight – or be singed.
Pulling out my wooden sword
Made with nails and with board
I swing with all my might
Swinging – through my fright.
I whistled to my stallion
Like the Duke and his battalion
Chasing them down the hall
This time you're mine! I call.

Suddenly, I graze the wall and fall.

I wince and they are gone
My ears are filled with song
A lullaby of sorts
No reason – and no retort
Alone and entirely me.

I glimpse from under my cover
In my heavy robe I now quiver
The hallway it has a glow
A whisper amongst the fog – it grows.
Frozen stiff I have become
Until the warm glow of the Sun
Only then I can rest
For it is darkness they obsess.

I close my eyes and fall into dream
Alone and entirely me.

christian school

stuffed in lockers

head flushed in toilets

rubber band welts on my arms

smacked in the back of the head

dropped head first into trashcans

lighter burns on my body

molested

held over the second story by my belt loops

face pressed into my food

kidney slaps

locked in bathrooms

locked in classrooms

tacks glued to my chair

fingers broken by the smashing of rocks

shoulder broken by being jumped after class

backpack stolen

drawings stolen

lunch stolen

ink poured on my favorite jacket

thrown on the ground in the hallways

thrown on the ground in the gravel

thrown on the ground in the parking lot

thrown on the ground in the cafeteria

never invited

left out

never picked – not even last

called a faggot

called a nobody

called a loser

called a weirdo

called a creep

jesus freak

spit on

spit on

spit on.

sure, I'd love to go back.

when did you say the reunion was?

he's buried in the backyard with a pair of my shoes

last summer
my sister
and i
sorted through
my old things
at my parents
place
high
in the fog
of the mountains

i came across
my old writings —
stories and
poetry
penned by the
teenage
version of me

piles of poems
describing

the loss of
my
childhood dog

tear stained
pages
telling
how much
it saddened me

that was some
really
depressing shit
to read

i was
suicidal over
that dog's
death

what
a weird
lonely kid
i was

these days
i'm trying
to do
a
decent job
not becoming
a weird
lonely man —
but damn do
i miss
that dog.

Of Ancient Clay

I have disconnected.

I am now but a passenger.

Simply moving through.

I observe.

I create.

I am unknown.

I am a part of the energy.

I see the molecules.

I feel the pulse from the center of the earth.

I am eternal.

I am distant.

I am love.

all of this madness for a cup of coffee

a busy
parking lot
near my house.
the coffee
shop
i
frequent.

every visit
the
same as
today,
five people
in their SUVs
(Party of one –
seats eight).
three of them
with a cell
phone
to their ears,
two of them
staring at

a smart phone

screen

six inches

from their

faces.

paying any

attention

to the

parking lot

war

but all

of them

creating it.

technology,

more distraction

than

salvation.

more dumbing

than

enlightening.

it'll take
another twenty
years
for society
to realize
that technology
should be
made to
enhance
not control
one's life.

and
by that
time it may
be too late.

the stupefying
may already
have seeped into
the genes
and mankind
will begin its
demise

and start
slipping back
into the
water
as hand
turns to fin
and gills
form behind
ears.

leaving me in
a parking lot
full of
fish
still trying
to park my car.

from high on my horse in a world of one

the writer
needs the poison
to be a writer

i don't need
the poison

which is why
they will
most likely
never
call me
a writer

i don't mind
though
i'm plenty of
other
things from
time to time
that they'll
never call me

i've never

needed them

the noise

poison

or the

numbing rhyme.

Money Better Spent at the Races

Poetry doesn't pay.

But I need it,

And so do you.

You need the rhythm

Like the race horse

Needs the water

After circling the track –

Every lap, same as the last.

You need the words,

The ones with rhythm,

To break up the music

Of everyday life.

You need poetry

But you won't pay –

And the three-legged horse

Will never win.

how to pay your bills

from morning
to night
i look up
through the moon
roof
and watch the
low-hanging
bellies
of airplanes
slingshot
over my head.

from morning
to night
i drive in
circles
airport to
downtown luxury
hotel,
downtown luxury
hotel to
airport —

one after the
other,
after the
other.

i've pocketed
26 dollars in tips
today
one dollar from
an old NFL running back
who was white
smelled of cigars
and carried himself
like a man who won
five Super Bowls –
he didn't win any.

five dollars from a
former Oakland Raider,
giant of a man
who answered his wife
in unintelligible
mumbles

and liked to hum
hip-hop beats under
his breath,
his hand swallowed my
entire right arm
when we shook.

20 dollars came
from a boxing promoter
who was famous
for billboarding Ali
and Frazier,
he even logged
a famous
Tyson bite.
he liked to scream
and curse
at his cell
phone.
i dropped he
and eight bags
off at
a mansion
in Buckhead –

i think he
gave me
a dollar
for each time
he screamed.

another airplane
flies above
taunting me to touch
its wings
as i sit
and circle
and
dream
of flying away
from this
merry-go-round
monotony.

One Sentence at a Time

As I pulled up the drive the moonlight poured
in through the sunroof.
Peggy Lee was singing *Days of Wine and Roses*.
I shut down the engine and let her finish.
I thought, *This song would be lovely on vinyl*.
I unlocked the door and headed upstairs
for a bottle of water.
Back down I went and out into the street.
I focused on my breathing to obtain relaxation
and a clear head for thinking.
I walked.
Thought.
Wrote things down on the walls of my mind.
I sang the verse to a song I wrote, last night,
over and over.
Out loud.
I pondered how one, brief, encounter could
spark such a thing.
I wandered onto the university that shares
the main road with my new home.
Soon after, I found myself on the baseball field
by way of an unlocked gate.

Standing at home plate, with nothing but the moon
to light the field, I began to daydream.
I took a few practice swings.
Then, accepted a pitch from the mound in front
of me and smacked it out of the park.
I ran the bases as if the game depended upon it.
When I returned to home plate, out of breath,
I chuckled at myself.
I loved the game.
Teamwork.
Being accepted.
Unfortunately, I wasn't molded to partake.
Or be accepted.
I stood there looking up at the lights –
memories flashed back.
I remember trying out for the team every year
in high school.
I shook my head and sadly laughed
as I also remembered being cut from the team.
Every year.
Just before the first game of the season.
I pulled out the drawer labeled
"Pieces of life that make me who I am"
and placed these memories back inside.

I left the ball field and headed out past
the soccer field, the tennis court, the gymnasium.
Walking down Granny White Pike,
I arrived at one of my favourite bookstores.
Looking in the window I smiled thinking
how great it was that I could walk here.
The littlest of things have always
made me the happiest.
I journeyed back through the campus
stopping to read a few placards
detailing moments of history.
I smiled again as I thought of how much
my love for history has grown.
I stumbled upon a perfect little white swinging bench
and made it my own for the next 30 minutes.
Aside from the crawlers of the night,
and the surrounding vegetation, I seemed
to be the only living organism out that evening.
Yet as time passed a couple walked by
arguing distinctively about their relationship.
He seemed miserable.
She, adamant.
I looked at the empty seat to my left
and mentally shrugged my shoulders.

Shortly after, an older gentleman flew by
on his bicycle.
Making a few rounds up and down ramps
he too seemed to be reliving his youth.
Soon, I was alone again.
Crickets sang and the damp air grew thicker.
Naturally, my thoughts turned back to love.
I was looking at a tree in front of me thinking
it seemed perfect for carving initials
enclosed by a heart.
I was brought back to when I was in Central Park
this past May having those same thoughts.
Different tree.
Different interests.
Knowing that this life was not mine to script
I stood and began to make my way back home.
Here I sit.
It's empty.
Quiet.
But for now I am content.

Lukewarm Coffee

Cold and loud
Yet
Peace is found
In the warmth
of Merton's pages

Snow is afoot
Yet
Chimneys birth soot
From the flats
Of English patrons

Lips crack dry
Yet
Winter's pricked sky
Brings Orion's light
To satisfied eye.

Magazine Queen

Perfectly chiseled
Green dress – new shoes
An angel walking
Among dust and fumes.

Seeking to save me
Wanting to set free
Longing to be
A patron of mercy.

Yet spiraled she down
Only to choose
Missing soul cleansing
By having had heart used.

Mouth begged but for a drink
From the chalice of truth
To fill her lost and lonely
Fountain of youth.

how to save a life

we were young
and foolish
and we wanted to meet girls,
my buddies also wanted to get wasted
but i just wanted to
talk to pretty girls.
one of the guys heard
of a house party
over here
over there
West Valley
East Valley
it made no matter
being 18 we said we were
at the house of the other for the night
and would stay out until the sun rose.

we made our way to a party
and were greeted
by a large Mexican man
as he came barreling out
of the house towards us.

he smashed his 40-ounce bottle

against the curb

and ran up to me

holding the sharp jagged end

against my throat screaming,

why did you fuck her, vato?!

at this point in my life

i hadn't fucked anybody,

or used that despicable vulgar word.

you've got the wrong guy, man!

i let out as he pushed the glass

into my neck –

i could feel the blood

begin to trickle down.

before he could do me in

Justin came from his side

of the car and slammed

the guy into the ground,

making sure he didn't get up.

that was the shortest amount

of time we ever spent at a party.

as we all piled back into the car
i thanked him for saving my neck
and told him that i owed him one.

years passed and
we were in New Mexico
at a shanty shack of a bar
somewhere outside of town
filled with women past
their prime,
biker gangs,
tequila
and karaoke –
a real Roadhouse affair.

i still wouldn't touch alcohol
and was really wanting to get out of there;
i seemed to always want to be leaving.

Justin was 13 shots to the wind
and propped up against the back wall
slobbering on a microphone in his hand
screaming the words to Cash's
Ring of Fire with a whiskey slur.

a woman of mammoth proportion
twice his heavy
mounted him as he fell over
into the corner and onto the wet floor –
she began licking his face
and laughing in-between slurps.

after quite a scuffle
i was able to force her to dismount by
holding a large pint of beer
in front of her face and yelling,
hey, hey! here, this is for you!
she followed the beer
as i set it down at the furthest table.

i ran over to Justin, who was twice my heavy,
grabbed his arms and drug him across
the wet dirty floor and out in the street.

as far as I was concerned
we were even.

the place with the neon
lights just off the highway

i was 19
do you remember
me?

they thought
it was funny
to kidnap
and drag me
inside that
den of
iniquity
where you
disrobed
for dollars
and drinks

i was
petrified
mortified
i could only

look into your

eyes

as you

swung

from side

to side

after your

number

you came

and sat

at our table

you resembled

Jewel

complete with

crooked smile

you were

easy

to talk to

you hated

the work –

it made

you cry

night after

night

i told you

i would take

you to

church

with me

you agreed

to go

but it only

made you

feel dirty

and incomplete

i would have

loved to see

their faces

if they found

out how

we met

where i picked
you up
with your
purse
full of
regret

i suppose i
was trying
to leave
the box
even then –
back when
i still cared
who was
adding up
my sin

i suppose
that was the
moment
that i began
to understand

that those

outside of

the box

were just

like

me.

Why the Whiskey

Making mistakes
In a stained world.
Trying to stay soft
When the machine pours cement.
Hiding in back alleys
Living under the best-selling Book.
Fighting for a change within
Before the light dwindles,
And hell comes chasing
Down my throat
Again.

Starspeak

You can't escape me.
For the stars
Spell out your sins.

Angelic Architect

How much control do you really have
In this game Of Mice and Men
How much of this is me
Or you moving my pen
Does it matter if I get it right
The who the why and the when
Do angels tally till the end
Or does drinking benevolence win
Leaving dust and wings to defend.

Bitter Wine

So fragile
So innocent
Perfection blended
No lament.
Years from now
Nothing will stay the same.

Beauty will leave
Along with friends
And family.
No one will know
Secrets that don't show
The ones only she will keep.
Tears in the night
A stage lit with lies
Nothing has stayed the same.

For she protected he
A lifetime of misery
Secrets feeding grief
Protection in the trees
Everything remains the same.

black ice

that snow
the piles left
shunned by the sun
remind me of
the streetwalkers
you know the ones
vixen of the night
once pure and fun
now melting away
in the shadows
done in
and undone.

Choked

Cigarettes living in my lung
No I did not smoke nary a one
For it was the girl
Who took hold of me
And into my throat
The dragon did breathe.
For a fortnight I choked
And another I hoped
That this was the end
Of the fire within
So to Confession I ran
To rid body of sin.
Leaving the booth
I tripped and I fell
Hitting my head
Oh the dizzying spell
From my knees did she lift
Head wrung as a bell.

The next thing I saw
Was the amber glow

How I arrived back here
I will never know.
Wrapped in her arms
Body entwined
She raised me close
Pressing her lips to mine.

she walks through walls

you had me scared,
a college girl
who writes poetry.

but you're not a college girl
writing poetry.

you're Dickinson's ghost –
hiding amongst
youth group soda drinkers.

Mary Magdalene in Ecstasy

She was soaked in religion
But I loved her still
She was married to the mob
White under darkened eyes
Mammoth structures of gold
Fastened to a thousand hills
Where the cattle all follow
Cutting their teeth
Every seventh day
Keeping their coin in pocket
Avoiding fountains
Avoiding a careless toss
And building
Always building.

If I could remove the stains
Splattered carelessly on the walls
If I could extract her soul
And save it for this life
For my life
I would.

She would be the queen
Of my idolatry
The vein that feeds
My sexuality
The moving picture show
On the pages
Of tattered books I read.

Her soul would move upon
The Eastern Winds
And brushes would stir the seas
Creating a masterpiece
For all to believe
And I would give foot to worshipping
To praising the created
Thus thumbing the creator
Adding another mark to my name.

For I am but a flawed being
A soul locked under key
An anchorless vessel seeking understanding
Seeking a harbor to knot myself upon
Seeking a place to release

Most assuredly explaining their need
To keep me on a leash
And far away from She.

stereotype disease

you are foremost
a soul
holding fast
to a spirit.
you are then
a human being
with a beating heart
full of life
and the strongest
of desires
to love.

you are then
how you treat others
then,
defined by character –
behind closed doors
and open ones,
this makes you
who you are.

then come the
things
like taste,
style and
charm.

and only
after
all of these
things
are you a
sexual preference
or
a
colour.

so —
when you look
at someone else,

what do you see first?

every hair on your head

if you had nothing
with which to identify by
would you still be who you are?
if all of the books
with which you relate
were caught up in a fire
and all of the music you've
collected through the years
were lost with the clothes
that give you taste and charm
and if you stood naked
as the day
in the dust
after dark
would you still be you?
would you still be set apart?

An Essay on Confidence

My gracious

You're so freaking loud.

With your boast

Of musical genius

And noteworthy prowess.

Your mouth moves at lengths

That run customers out.

To hear you speak

One would think

You a god,

Or demi – at least.

Is that the ghost of Elvis,

Morrison

Or Lennon

Wrapped in fleece?

You said your name so loud

I couldn't help

But remember it.

When I arrived home

I googled you.

Apparent it was
That running your mouth
Is the best thing you can do.

Music so awful
That I'd rather
Listen to the shrieks
Of tiny woodland creatures
Burning.
Your branding
And design
So pathetic
I believe it to be
Created with
PC Paint
In 1983.
Good grieving
Why are you here?
Who told you it was
A good idea?

Somewhere,
A village is missing
An accountant.

god pity thee

who you are
is who you are
when you are alone.

and if you are
never alone
you are no one –
just a reflective pool
for those you are
always with.

you are not
who you tell
them you are,
you are not
who you act
as you play
the part –

you are not
those stupid tight
pants

that lame fashion
bag
that shit haircut
or the vest
and silver rag.

you are not
the politics
that you spit
or the news
that you speak.

you are not
a religion
not a god
that you preach.

you are
who you are
when you are
alone

and if you

are

never alone

then

god pity thee.

Solitaire Checkmate

I am the king
of creating
and not the way you think
I make a mark
and build a scene
then simply
lean
press play.

The mark is here
again tonight
now all to do
is wait
swaying left
then sliding right
now pause to stop
stare
delay.

Drinking in is
necessary

as is reflecting
on the hour
I search now for
the moment
to softly interject –
connecting lines
and adding dots
to find the perfect
rest.

The mark has drifted
out of sight
has slipped
as I protest –
for after all
I created thee
a mark to have
and hold
one to move
in and out
of the need
in my beautiful
endless deep.

So why am I left

begging

that which I create

to come

and take

these eyes

of want

and lay

a world

of pain.

Healthy Words For The Son That Isn't Mine

I was there when –
you were growing inside the womb
you took your first breath
you released your first cry
you opened your eyes.

I was there when –
you learned to hold yourself up
you started to crawl
you first saw the sky
you first said a word.

I was there when –
you took your first step
saw your first bug
caught your first butterfly
fell in love with the dirt outside.

I was there to –
change your diapers
feed you from a bottle
feed you from a spoon

rock you to sleep in my arms
hold you through the night.

I am here now as you –
discover the world
expand your mind
grow from boy to man
decide who you are
when to take a stand.

***

From where I now sit
I can tell you things that will –
ease the hardest day
teach you how to live
show you what a real man is
how to make a difference
how to save your soul.

First, the popular kids will –
all end up overweight
peak at 18

work at a dead end job
be miserable at 25
have addictions they can't kick
always be insecure.

Second, you don't need to —
talk about the sluts of the big screen
to fit it and prove you aren't gay
look at porn to be cool
or make yourself feel like a man
tell dirty jokes and get with the girls,
these things make a weak
cheap
man out of you
and only chip away at your soul.

You don't need to —
hang out in dirty places with shallow
older kids who want sheep to follow,
you are not anyone's pet
you do not have a leash around your neck
if you are trying to fit in
it means you will never fit in.

Third, a real woman wants –
a man who is unique
a man who is sensitive and in touch
is not afraid to talk about his feelings
will fight for himself
and most importantly for her.

A real woman wants –
a man who has passion
a man who doesn't follow the crowd
a man who stands for something
a man who seeks the spiritual –
believes in things beyond himself.

Fourth, when life is unbearable –
stop and count slowly to ten
put on a good song and sing along
go outside
breathe in the fresh air
take note of something small
a blade of grass, a tree or a bird whistling.

When life is unbearable –
think of someone besides yourself

pray

consider the raven

step away from the situation

remember what you thought was

a big deal five years ago

and how it's laughable now.

Lastly, know that I know who you are –

the kid who loves the earth

the kid who loves insects

the kid who loves his pets

turtles, frogs and fish.

I know who you are –

the kid who loves to draw

the kid who loves to build things

the kid who reads as much as I do

the kid who fell in love with Shakespeare

at the age of ten.

I know who you are –

the kid who has a heart of gold

the kid who like his Uncle wants to

be accepted and loved

the kid who loves his Mom, Dad,
Sister and Grandparents
the kid who loves me –
the kid who I need.

Departure/Arrival

Just before daybreak
I sat on the runway
the clouds lay heavy
upon what remained of the darkness
as I peered out my window
I could see a touch of the sun
beginning to do the same thing
it has done since time began
as I sat in the silence
of mine own thought
I fought back the tears

she would never see another sunrise
its earthly glow
will never again paint her face
with its warmth

as I was lifted
at great speed
the darkness was left behind
for what I could not see

from underneath
was revealed high above the clouds

what mine eyes beheld
was almost too intense for my earthly shell
to comprehend
more beauty than imagined
magnificently brushed
just a few steps in
this staircase to heaven

for my view is limited
stifled by this stunted window frame
my perception prohibited
as I still sit in human display
yet as for her
mere mortal words could never capture
the visions
inhaled on her journey
the combination
of all the imaginations in the world
would fail to come close
to what her eyes have beheld

for the eternal sunrise

is hers to dance in

both now

and forevermore.

[for Nik – may you ever rest in peace]

Afterlife

Tonight, in the deepest chamber of my mind,
I told her that I loved her.

I told her that I still couldn't understand why she
had to go.

I asked her if she remembered sitting on
Grandpa's swing together;
laughter and horse play in his yard.

I told her that I have been stuck since that fated
October day.
As if time has stood still.

As if I haven't aged a bit, and neither has she.
I can't explain why – yet, I felt that she could hear me.

a tree for molly

i oft' ponder why the trees
so full of life and lush,
shed their clothes of orange and green
along with underbrush.
doing so with winter's approach
days before first snow,
a season growing the perfect coat
only to let it go.

falling like leaves

there sits an
old woman
she has a book
a cup of coffee
and a worn
blue cane

she is wrapped in
a long green
woolen pea coat

she sits
grabs her head
stares into
nothing

she tries to read
grabs her head again
stares into
nothing

she shakes as
she takes small
sips of her coffee

she smiles at me
as she catches
my eyes studying

i too smile

i wish i had
the power
to give her
50 years back
to ease her
of the aches
to free her
from the cane

but i can
do nothing
but grow old
myself

so i sit
grab my head
and stare
into
nothing.

January Sky

Looking out from the Observatory
Just across the way
A wooden swing hangs from atop the porch.
Through the swirling snow
I see it sway, ever so gently.
The weathered house sits
Unattended and un-lived in
As it has for a decade now —
Yet, I can't help but see it
As it was a hundred years ago.
Fresh paint on the shutters;
Newly stacked bricks
Making up the outer walls
And a family sitting together
On the porch
Watching the same sun
Provide a haunting glow
Through winter skies
Covering green grass
With crystal snow.

And there the wooden swing hangs
From atop the porch
Swaying gently with the wind.
And I can't help but think,
Perhaps it has never stopped.

sad thoughts for a beautiful morning

this morning
i woke up
to the snow
all around me,
everything
was white
and calming.

i went into the bathroom,
brushed my teeth
at the sink
and put a small
piece of plastic
over each eye.
i went back
to the window
and saw the snow,
without the blur.

lacking road
maintenance
there will be

no leaving
the house
today.

i went into the kitchen,
put the coffee on.
i went to
the record
player –
put Sinatra on.
not young
happy Frank
but old
blue eyes,
the one
from '73 –
telling them
to send in
the clowns.

i grabbed
Neruda
and Bukowski

from my
nightstand
and thumbed
the pages –
stopping at
interesting
titles and
digesting
just a few.

Neruda fuels
my lust for love.
Bukowski
tells me to
keep it simple,
honest and straight
from the hip.
both help
me
release my
voice –
while everyone
else
makes me

feel as though
i'm not good
enough
and should
keep my mouth
shut and
my pen dry.

i walked
over to the
couch,
sat down
and stared out
the window.

folding my hands
under my chin
i wondered
who i should listen
to today.

perhaps I should
listen   .
to the writers

because they
are dead.

the dead can't
hurt you
like the living
can.

Coffee in Lebanon

It is mid day
I sit
in a small
coffee shop
in Lebanon
enjoying my cup
full.

This shop
was difficult
to find.

I say –
"Not many places
to get a
cup of coffee
here in Lebanon."

She says – "No,
they all close
within a few
months.

This one will
too."

"Sad" – I say.
"Who doesn't
drink coffee?"

I sit
taste my coffee.
It is good.
Hits the spot.
What with the
snow on the ground
and all.

A twenty-something
walks in –
"Are you hiring?"
He says.

"No." She says,
looking down
at the ground.

Smalltown, USA
That's just
the way it
is.

I read poetry –
A posthumous
author's work.
Always the dead,
never the
living.
The living
write too
arrogantly for
me.

Like the world
Should listen.
Like the
people owe
it to them.

I write
for therapy.

I write
because
it calms me.

No one should
listen.

The world
owes me
nothing.

I take another
drink.
The low-
signal radio
speaks of War.
Foreign soil.

I think of
soldiers,
humans,
lying in mud
crawling
in filth.

Dying for
others.

Fighting for
Greed.

Dying in
mud.

I sit
under my
wide-brimmed
fedora.
wrapped in
my
wool coat.
Drinking warmth
from a
cup.

Why am I
so lucky?
Why do I
struggle with

menial things
while they
go hungry.

While they
die
in shallow
graves they
dug to
survive.

I can't
take
another drink.
My thoughts
invade
my reality
and I leave
to think
about something
I haven't
even seen.

a picture of a man staring at nothing

outside the window
it looks like
what I'd imagine
war torn Moscow
to feel —
in the dead
of winter
in the dead
of romance.

inside pretty young minds
shape their beings with
books, books their parents
have paid far too much for.

inside the stench of cigarettes
flow through a constant
opening and closing door —
attacking my weak lungs.

I pull my checkered scarf
above my mouth
in an attempt to filter the poison.

I think about anything and everything.
there is work waiting, money I need to collect
bills I need to pay ...

but I'd much rather sit and think.
so I do.

and outside the war-torn skies
grow darker still
as they spit upon the land
the purest of snow.

the purging white,
the earths cold blanket.

today's reset button.

What Dreams May Come

When it had begun we acted as if it were a game.
Stay out of sight.
Be an apparition.

Soon —
They found us.

Some ran.
Others hid.

Most were taken.

Myself and a few others managed to remain unseen.
Until the next night.

We were captured and marched off
to a giant compound.

They were Chinese soldiers.
None spoke a word.
Not even to each other.
We were in our own country.

But they were here.

We were taken into a large chamber room.
Like something out of a post-apocalyptic film.

When I walked in I saw some of the others
that were with us.
Just the day before.
People were stacked one on top of the other.
Like loaves of bread on the supermarket shelf.
Some were crying.
Others were dazed.
Those who were with me piled in.
As if they knew the routine.
They began to stack themselves amongst the others.

One by one.

I made my way into the middle.
Constantly thinking of a way out.

I'm getting us all out of here.
I said aloud.

I made eye contact with a girl of about
25 years of age.
There was something very familiar in her gaze.
Her hair was cut short, like a child's.
Not shaven, yet short and choppy.

I looked around the room.
All the women had their hair cut short.

The lights seemed to fade on and off.
In rhythm with a distant humming sound.

I slid my way in next to the girl.
I kept looking at her face.
I kept looking into her eyes.
They were very calming to me.
Large blue eyes taking me in.

A younger kid to my right –
That I remembered from the day before.
Was frantically asking me if I knew him.
If I knew what his name was.
When the last time I saw him was.

I said.

Yes, I know you.

I saw you yesterday.

I couldn't tell if he had been drugged.

Or if it was sheer fright that had a hold of him.

Seconds after speaking to him.

He laid back.

His eyes left mine.

And he was gone.

Just like that.

I checked for a pulse.

Nothing.

Again, I said aloud.

I'm going to get us all out of here.

I looked to the front of the compound,

near the door we came in.

Some stood with arms raised and hands held high.

Swaying back and forth.
As if they heard music.

Suddenly, I heard a loud crack.
The lights went out.

I awoke to the sound of birds singing.
And sunlight pouring in through my window.

*[26 august 2009 – written immediately
after awaking from this dream]*

1911 Love

There is a woman
who lives across
the street
who was born
in the year
1911.
One could assume
that she is
made of steel.
She is up with the birds
from morning till night
and she walks about
better than most
twenty years her junior.

There is another woman
who lives to my left
who is a thirty-something
mother of two.
She visits with the
elderly woman daily

sometimes bringing
her twin boys to see her.

And sometimes,
like today,
she goes by herself
to share simple moments.
Right now she is blowing
bubbles, like I used to do
when I was just a child.
They are both laughing
and enjoying the simplicity
of it all.

In this I see the purity
that still exists in this
hardened world
and in this I see Love.

the brave

disconnected
when they said
it was rubbish
when they
took your name
and added stain
as if
it were
the remains
of a
sun-bleached
poster
that read
lost dog
no reward.

i found
it to be
the brilliant
start to
another
side –

honesty

a thing to pride

but you

left

and called

the dog

a puppy

publicly.

to that i

can't blame

i am still

stuck here

and I feel

exactly the

same.

i think it's

time to

make another

even if

the response

will repeat.

your army

is greater

now

and

your teeth

are gold –

do it for

Brando

Hunter

the Three

do it for

a kid

from Phoenix

who is

still seen

as the

remains

of a

sun-bleached

poster

that reads

lost dog

no reward.

a lesson in waiting

i wanted to
keep
my arms
clean
in case
i finally
got that
good job
acting

but the
good job
never came
only the lame
ones that
no one
wants to
tell anyone
about

all those plays
and stage
performances
done under a
cross
or on one
bleeding for
the lost
or those
extra roles
for $50
a day

"here, hold
this briefcase,
now walk in front
of the camera."

"CUT!"

"could you walk
a little
slower?"

"ACTION!"

the good job
never came
so
after a
long while
i said
screw it
and started
using my arms
as reminders
of where
i've been
or where
i want
to go

i think
i prefer
the ink
on my arms

to the

good job

but then again,

i've never

had

the good job.

the owl and the talisman

your death
has taught me
that there are those
who are un-teachable

those who will never change
those who will live their
entire lives
living inside
of a three-ring circus
with a burning big top
tied to the legs
of their offspring
children who will never
run nor hide

who among us
is not selfish
let them cast the first
die

who among us

knows

what truth and light

hides behind the

veil of the

after-life

the owl

now knows

as she casts

that teachers stare

with raised brow

over horn-rimmed

glasses

and sees from all

sides

the owl

is now

living in the

eastern trees

keeping watch

both day and night

twitching her eye
at the un-teachable
and casting
the first die.

Never Look Yourself in the Eye

I've been told a simple tale
of my great-grandfather, Perry.
A man who I never
consciously met; a man who
I believe only met me once when
I was a 20 pound mass of skin
and soft bone.

It's said that he never felt old
never let it catch him
and never saw it coming.
Until one day when he paused
to look at his reflection in the mirror.
To his surprise he had no idea who
the wrinkled and frail faced man
staring back at him was.
And as the tale goes, the man
in the mirror looked back with
a slow wink and said,
"gotcha."
And would you believe it,

Perry fell dead right then
and there.

From what I can surmise
this must explain why
I spend little to no time
looking directly into the mirror.

history repeating

coughing again
two weeks ago i was sick —
had the strep throat.
i went to the clinic
and the doctor gave me two shots
right in the ass
followed by ten days worth
of meds.

now i'm sick again
miserably so —
fever, sore throat, head jolting
lightning bolt coughs of pain
and aches everywhere.
modern medicine —
the American money farm with a
revolving door, where the farmers
don't care to know your name.
just a number
with a dollar sign attached.

I am a Jellyfish

I wake up.

I am floating in a body of water.

I am a Jellyfish.

The day moves slow,

A week must have passed by now.

I look at the clock

John Wayne says it's 2 p.m.

I spend the day with James Dean

And Sherlock Holmes.

I go to the store to pick us up some milk

Brake lights resemble stoplights

Just closer to the ground.

I should have taken the horse

I don't have a horse.

I drive slow.

I'm home.

It's only 3 p.m.

It feels like a month has passed.

I pass out.

I wake up.

It's 6 p.m.

Where am I going?

I walk in late.

Everybody stares.

Is something on my face?

Where are my pants?

I want to run.

I sit.

I mumble nonsensical whims.

People chuckle.

Where are my pants?

I am a Jellyfish.

I'm home.

It's 10 p.m.

Why isn't it colder outside?

It should be December.

I pick up my shoes

To return them to Blockbuster.

But that doesn't make sense.

Where are my car keys?

I am a Jellyfish.

I shouldn't drive,

I should swim.

The Ape With Fins

I am constantly evolving
like a monkey to a man
I do all to keep swimming
like a fish growing hands.

Asymmetrical

I'm glad
I'm not pretty
So pretty
That society
Wants to put
Me in a cage
And collect money
From people
Who want to
Look at me
Through glass.

Best Compliment/ Worst Compliment

"I'd really like to talk to him.
I think he should have been
born a thousand years ago."

"You remind me of Lars,
from *Lars and the Real Girl*,
I just kept thinking of you
the entire movie."

And He Begat

I see his genes
As they form around my waist.
At 33
It's starting to get to me.

When he threw papers,
Under the early morning moon,
His waistline would shrink.

Maybe I should
Throw papers, too.

The Boxer With Hands Tied

At 35 I am finally strong
enough
to fight anybody.

The problem is
at 35
I am too smart
to fight anyone.

I have missed
my opportunity
to get into some
really good
nose busting
scraps.

Grey Knit Hat

You see,

Linus had his blanket

And I,

This grey knit hat.

Under it

I keep a mess

Of tangled

Tri-coloured hair,

And a mind

That feels protected.

It's absurd,

Yet warm.

in my honest opinion

you look
soooooo
much better
with your hair
cut short like that.
sincerely,
everyone.

dear everyone,
i'm growing
it back out
because I prefer
it long.
sincerely,
me

van gogh's to-do list

[x] cut off ear

[ ] give ear to rachel

The Week a Storm Blew In

He walked in
turned on the TV
Set the remote down
saying,

"I guess I don't
have the patience
for television
anymore."

Then he walked
out to the deck,
and then he walked back
to the couch,
sat down
and stared at the TV.

Volume so low
you couldn't hear anything
above a mumble.

I looked up
from my work
and said,

"Do you even know
what you are watching,
or did you just
turn the TV on
for the hell of it?"

He replied,

"I don't know,
I am just looking
at the people."

Cocoon

The butterfly

must

first

be suffocated

before

it

is

free

to fly.

Spinning Plates

Life is too short

to try

and

glue together

broken plates

that were

cheap

in

the

first place.

Virtue

As the leaf
takes its
time
finding
the ground
so
must
I.

Decibel

Sometimes
the silence
is the
loudest thing
in
the
room.

Pause

Life
is
so
much more
than what
you do
or
do not
believe.

Bonfire

You can
burn
all of
the
pictures
but they
still stay
in
your
head.

LOSING
SIGHT
OF THE
SHORE

Siksiká Ohkó

I found a fell tree
twenty-nine paces
from the water's edge.

I made the day turn night
as I created a womb
inside of the great white oak
as a hatchet extended
past the reach of my left hand.

The darkness surrounded
on all sides while I
birthed a fire using the life
left inside of my lungs.

The burning coals
served three-fold as they
provided warmth, light
and softened the womb inside.

While the fire burned into dawn
blending with the horizon line
I shaped both bottom and sides
of the mighty fallen oak.

Leaving the blackened womb
to burn with the morning sun
I took to the surrounding wood
gathering pre-amber pitch
and boughs with which to spread.

Upon my return
to the water's edge
and the freshly carved oak
complete with hardened spread
I heard the whispering wind speak
Ohkó it is time to leave.

Filling my chest
With the breeze of the sea
I took to bended knee
thanking the earth for safe keeping
kissing the soil
leaving soft prints of my feet.

Exhaling as I slid the mighty oak
across the water's edge
I entered its womb
pushing off from the sand
creating ripples ahead.

Now complete and entirely me
I turned to face
the open sea
through the fog I created doors
leaving the days of yore
losing sight of the shore.

a separation

on the open sea
the horizon
before me –
it is as if
the sky
was cut
from A to B,
and out of
its stomach
bleed the
waters
that fill
the deep.

[25 November 2011, Gulf of Mexico.
Sailing from Ft. Myers to Key West, Fla.]

Mi Isla

As I lie
Naked
On the beach
The sky
Is half open
Revealing
Her vast
Display of
Sparkling diamonds.

The other half
Veiled behind
Heavy clouds
Ever so oft
Dropping rain
Upon my skin.

I lie here
With candlelight
With books
Of wisdom

And with
Pen and
Parchment
I deliver words
As quickly
As they slip
From my
Loosened tongue.

For because
There is no
Moon tonight
I steal much
From her supple
Air

Filling my
Senses
With the scents
Of angels.

No harm may
Befall me
This night

For the sweet
Scented ones
Dance about
My cloth-less
Existence.

Tonight
Love is a
Red grape
That pours
Smoothly down
My throat
And kisses
Upon my mind
With such
A gentle touch.

One that would
Make the most
Bonded of lovers
Quiver with
Jealousy.

For I move with

The rhythm of

The waves

I speak with

The voice

Of the

Enchanted

And

As I lie

Naked as I came

I will fall

Into an

Ancient slumber

And dream

The things

That the strongest

Of men

Would beg

At bended knee

To be saved

From having

To behold.

For my eyes

For my soul

Have journeyed

To places

Unknown

To marks

Never inked

Upon maps

Of old

It is here

That I

Am king

It is here

That my soul

Sings

Upon

Unencumbered

Wings

And it is

Here

That I

Do far

More

Than simply

Dream.

[November 2011, Dry Tortugas.
Alone on an island 90 mi. from Havana]

To Be Tossed at Sea

I give my dreams
To the sea
For I fear
God
No longer
Hears me.

Whatever
Comes back
Be it this
Or
Be it that
I'll force
Mind
To know
It is
Meant
To be had.

*[December 2010, Atlantic Ocean. Gave a message
in a bottle to the sea — Ocracoke Island, N.C.]*

The Simple Things

I watched a leaf fall
With more grace than ever seen
So slowly
So divine
So simple and serene

I watched with intent
As it touched upon the water
Landing without a splash
No interruption, no bother

Oh, how quickly
Was this moment taken from me
As it rushed down the river
Captive in the stream

I turned to follow with my eyes
To see just where it went
I caught a glimpse

Made a wish

And away the leaf was sent.

[27 September 2009, Radnor Lake.
on my weekly fall hike – Nashville, Tenn.]

A Prayer of Query

Am I meant to have and to hold
Dare I dream to pen stories untold

What am I to make of this
These feelings that I miss
Where am I to go with this
These captivating thoughts of bliss

Is this mere perception
Am I lost in reflection
Reflection of years untold
Or things to come, things to unfold

I seek a dawning of new understanding
Patient – void of reprimanding
Wrap me up in arms outstretched
Longing to learn, lacking catch
A bottomless pool filled with un-condition
An empty pool void of remission
Eyes that need not
To glance back – to give more thought

Love given, not bought
Peace living, not sought.

[21 May 2009, Central Park. wandering the city,
stopping for thought – Manhattan, N.Y.]

The Tower of Babel and a Camera

Eyes of blue lightness
German tongue
Presence electric
Longing for some

Sing to me softly
Breath in my lung
Find me tomorrow
On morning dove

From the top of the world
Few words were spun
On towers of metal
Under blazon sun.

*[March 2008, Empire State Building. absorbing the
city, meeting someone new — Manhattan, N.Y.]*

Park Bench Carvings

Here I sit
dreaming
of
Love.

One day
she'll
find
me,
someday
she'll come.

[21 May 2009, Central Park. daydreaming,
leaving my mark – Manhattan, N.Y.]

[car 4]

start stop

come go

where is the next

no one knows

love leave

love again

come sit

feel descend

embrace depart

hold take

let

go

need

perfect

art

live

die.

[April 2009, subway train.
people watching – Manhattan, N.Y.]

Without a Stamp

Argentina streets

A monument of mimicry

Women with eyes of want and kind.

Enchanting dance of trance

Press play – then rewind.

A bridge to be shared

With postcards never sent

And I give up Love – for Lent.

[April 2009, Avenida 9 de Julio.
taking it all in – Buenos Aires, Argentina]

A Ghost of a Girl

I stand and
watch the sun
rise over Atlanta
from the sixth floor
of the Waverly
the colours shoot
across the sky
like exploding cans
of paint.

finding its way
through the clouds
the piercing orange
sun throws its light
against the windows
of the glass towers
like a prism
connecting the buildings
one to another.

it is going to be

another long

cold day of work

and if I don't get to see

her tonight

I must soak this in

because it will be

the only

beauty

in my day.

*[January 2011, Waverly Hotel. working 16-hour
days & odd jobs to make ends meet — Atlanta, Ga.]*

from hollywood, with love

a city so warm
full of acceptance and charm
if you've got a pretty face.

elegance and champagne
fast cars and fast lanes
if you've fallen from grace.

i should pack up now
and leave this town
back to the simpleton's place.

[September 2002, the Boulevard. watching the
madness on the streets – Hollywood, Calif.]

the city of angels

i was kindly
offered
a place to
stay
in the wealthy
hills
of stardom
and fame

i was three
weeks
late
on account
of an emergency
surgery —
a couple of knife
swipes
to save my
young life

i drove
through the
lonely desert
from dusk
until
midnight
arriving
good well
and fine

i found
the hidden key
set down my
guitar
aired out
my
bed roll
hung a few
shirts
and went back
down the
hill to find
a
hot meal

when i
returned
to the
one room
guest house
a welcoming
note
was taped
to the door –

squater,
i don't know
who the hell
you think you are
but if you
aren't immediately
gone i will
have you arrest...

before i could
finish reading

footsteps behind

me

turned into

a hairy shirtless

angry man

who didn't

utter a word

as i tried to

explain

he just kept on

pointing at

the long

winding staircase

up to the

exit

of his

hillside estate

i threw my

shirts in

my bed roll

grabbed

my guitar

and made my

way
back up the
long
winding staircase

after sitting
in my predicament
for a length
of time
i decided the
beach
would be
just as good
of a place
to sleep so
i made my
way to
the low-lit living
boardwalk

as i was shuffling
along
footsteps behind
me
turned into
two crazy-
eyed
transients
who whispered
into my ear –

We're going to
eat you alive
little boy

welcome to
Los Angeles,
i thought

in my new
predicament
i decided
to walk

instead of
sleep
that night.

*[September 2002, small diner. living out
of my car — Hollywood, Calif.]*

human pantheon

captivated by your beauty
the moment our eyes embraced,
your smile was uplifting
a vacation of sheer grace.

live in my mind for a moment
decorate the walls with joy —
feel my heart, does it still beat?

you are the kind to fall for; die for,
the silence of lovely i greet.

*[24 October 2005, Terminal 6. fresh face, the idea
of letting someone new in — St. Paul, Minn.]*

Wine and Loathing in Winter

I pulled into
the hotel
around 10:30
this evening,
the bar was closed.
After dumping
my luggage
I took to the
side-streets
to find sanctuary
and commune with
a glass of wine.

The red of
the thermometer
sought hibernation
as the wind
took heavily
to my face;
each pore
receiving it's
own needle –

in and out with
each passing gust.

Death
by acupuncture.

Three blocks up,
on Walnut,
I ducked into
a wine bar —
bearing no name.
I slid into a spot
without a stool
and asked for
the Cabernet.
I paid with cash —
I too
bore no name
tonight.
The selection
was horrible,
the wine
eight bucks
and salty.

But who's
complaining –
it's backwoods
Asheville
and I needed
the warmth.

I received
eleven sets
of eyes as
I made my way
to a seat
by the window.
*"Must not be
from 'round
these parts,"*
each one read.

In the
background
Percy Sledge
was belting out
the only decent

version of
When a Man
Loves a Woman.

Taking off my
jacket and scarf,
being enticed
by the words
of the song,
I thought –
who would I
say I most likely
loved tonight?

Picking up my
phone I sent
a text to
the first girl
who came to mind.
She's the one
whose eyes I loved
to see looking
deep into mine –

between kisses,
as she'd
bat her lashes.
Exonerating her
soul
with those dark
brown eyes,
further confusing mine.

Is that how I
defined loving
someone?
Based on a look –
a glance that
would sell?

My text read,
Are you happy?
Seconds later
I received,
No.
Birthed from
an insecure
internal place

I wrote,
Do you
miss me?

My screen lit
with the word,
Yes.

Then,
in schoolboy
fashion,
I typed out,
Miss other
guys too?
Instantaneously
the reply came back,
Ughhh,
you're dumb.
I sat for
a moment
then said,
What is the
point of this
grinding life?

My screen sat
dark – motionless,
without a response.

I could only
assume
she went back
to her beer
and forgot that
she missed me.

I set my phone
down – leaving
my world
to study those
around me.
Most notable
were the loud
obnoxious
laughs of
heavy-bottomed
blondes –
craving attention

worse than a

donkey in heat.

Next to them

a sadly

dressed

twenty-something

male

spoke of

his 401(k)

and an

extra he knew

in the film

Transformers.

Doing his best

to mask the

fact that

he was

not interesting —

only furthering Science.

The first

Darwinian

discovery,

his pants

peeling out

in the back – like
an unwrapped gift.
Displaying dopily
that his belt missed
a few loops.

A couple
to my right,
along the window,
were holding
hands – as the
man was doing
his best
to persuade the woman
that he
had her
best interest
in mind.
*"You're all I
care about."*
As he guzzled
his third beer.
Following with

words weaker yet,
"I'll send her
a text straight-away
and tell her
she's out."
The woman
rolled her eyes
then placed them
on me.
Watching as I
gently swirled the
wine in my glass.
I studied her
through the
reflecting window.
All the while
he was attacking
his smart phone
with dumb thumbs,
sticky with beer.

I nodded to
a homeless man
crossing in front

of the window,
leaving her eyes
for his.
What a sad
cold night
to be walking
the streets
scraping change
for a few sips
of whiskey.
If I were
any better off
I'd have bought
him his next
watery blanket.
I played out
the reactions
of the bar
patrons
had I
brought him
in to share
a drink
with me.

My screenplay
would have been
comical
with a twisting
life lesson —
consisting of
tears and
handholding
at the end.
A real
Schindler's List
moment.
"With this whiskey
I could have
saved one more."

I turned off
the reel-to-reel,
took one last
swallow
and stood up
to dress and
hand myself over
to winter's

tempered bosom.
Sliding my glass
to the bartender
I smiled and said,
"Merry Christmas."

See, I'm not all
stone and Sherlock.
I thought,
as I
pushed the door
against the wind.

Back outside
all depth of mind
departed as
I turned into
an animal
desperately
seeking shelter –
moving swiftly
down
side-streets.

Once back
inside hotel walls
I stumbled through
the darkness
and fell into bed.
Sleep and warmth
washed over me
passing
cold and thought
as night
turned to day.

[24 December 2010, Christmas Eve.
stopping over for the night — Asheville, N.C.]

Dare I Write It?
[I fear, I must.]

I've got to escape

This place.

This beautiful

Quaint

Charming place.

This town of creativity,

Trite as it may be.

Where every one can say

They're just like me.

Sixteen guitars on every corner.

Every one a singer,

A songwriter.

An author.

A self-employed

Self-absorbed

Socialite.

Poetic and creative

In their own rite.

Dressing up

To avoid being

Dressed down.

Going out
To avoid
Being settled and sound.
Introspection.
A mere painting
To appear as pretty within.

Here,
In this place,
My hand of skill,
My mind
Of power and will,
My Renaissance
And proverbial appeal
Lie completely mundane.
As straight as
A western Kansas highway.
As obnoxious as
A steady
Dripping
Faucet.

I've got to escape
This race.

Defined not by colour

But by

One's place

On the ladder.

A ladder so small

That it ought not matter.

Each and all

A proclaimed Christ follower

Of the Modern Era

In type.

Sheep without brains

Clinging to the Right.

Right as black and white.

Like day,

Like night.

No room to tread the dawn,

No space for twilight.

Making Faith trendy

To appear relevant; spread hype.

Yet comically, five years behind

And thirty billion spent

With receipts out of sight.

Heavenly kingdoms

With earthly thrones

Roving Jaguars
Extravagant homes
And a Starbucks inside
Every one of God's living catacombs.

I've got to escape
This race.

This blinded
Self-loving,
Self-seeking
Race.
For I would never serve
A god of trend
As shallow as
What type of jacket is in.
A god as hip
As a haircut sought in November.
Only to be mocked
With photos on top
Of stacks come next December.
Reverence turned to joke,
Clues missed
By common folk.

I choose to break bread
And drink red
In the solace
Of the open sky
Walls removed
To keep purity alive.
Among the branches
Of trees
I confide.
Stay away,
If you're asking,
For souls to take side.

I've got to escape
This place.
This beautiful
Picturesque
Place.

As I ride this time-machine,
This slow moving steampunked machine,
The second hand ticks
To reveal a dying being.

What will be left

To reflect

The man that is me

If I don't escape

If

I don't leave.

If

I keep ear to rail

For She.

Now a mere metaphor

For the Venus unseen.

In search

I grow old.

As the attic dust folds

Stocked heavily with mold.

The odor

From the scrolls

Tainted with abused tales

From suits

Who forget to inhale.

I've got to escape

This place.

For this town

Will not see me

Nor will the time-machine

Wait for me

And God

Will no longer

Move me.

[10 December 2010, Fido Coffee Shop.
fed up with the bullshit — Nashville, Tenn.]

the christian thing to do

i was traveling
with
a young Christian
performer
and
after the
show
we were
invited to
a small
house party

these sort of
things
were always like
The
Twilight Zone
meets
Dazed and Confused
with a side
of
religious wall-hangings

the place was
full of
stench
filth
and
cheap alcohol

the
barefoot ones
began to pass
around the herb
i refused
quietly
with
the subtle raise
of my hand
and when it
arrived
at the side
of the young
Christian
he too refused
making a
grandiose

comical scene
preaching
against
the way he
used to be
with a fifth
beer in his hand
proclaiming
that Jesus
had set him
free

two years
later
i heard
that he had
been running
around on
his wife
thusly
impregnating
a young
groupie

to which i
subtly raised
my hand
scratched my temple
and thought
to myself,
he should have
just smoked
the weed.

[Winter 2009, Colorado Springs, Colo.]

Under the Road

Queens and dreams

Filling my ears

Abandoning my fears

Pale hot sun

Sergeant Pepper and a gun

Lonely hearts

Half dead guitars

Sickly singers

Promoters and dead ringers

At the end of the day

Tomorrow awaits

And today

Is undone.

[24 March 2006, interstate
headed towards Jacksonville, Fla.]

figure 8

the stench of cheap hotels
and easy women
morning alarm bells ringing
leaving again
for the first time.

alone in part
together in mind
satisfied

wash away the window stain
everything left behind
memories of tomorrow
where the future
is a bright white light –

or so i'm told.

[March 2006, on the road – Tampa, Fla.]

two singers; one known, one treading water

we were on
the road
somewhere between
Alabama
and nowhere
in a rented
Cadillac.

i was driving.
i was always driving.

he turned to me
as a father to a son
and said,
"stop worrying about
the girl. with
guys like us the
girls will always
be there."

*[April 2006, on the road – driving
from Nashville, Tenn. to Atlanta, Ga.]*

Wave Upon Wave

I lie
on this
island
and watch
the clear
blue water
fold into
itself
with each
landing
upon the shore.

I want it
to tell me
something
I want it
to breathe
for me
I want it to
speak
for me.

It
is purer
than I,
and always
will be,
for it
comes and
goes
yet ever
stays
just the same –
never changing
never
to blame.

It never
fears
what is
inside,
what it
releases
upon the shore
nor what

the future
brings.

There is never
a bad day
nor a
friend
turned enemy.

There are
mysteries
left free
to keep
in the
dark
belly of
the deep.

There are beautiful
hidden things
exposed
only
to those
who will seek.

It is loved

it is feared

but it does

not feel

these things.

It is simple

it is serene

it is always

in motion

and

it is

always

living

in my dreams.

[27 November 2011, alone on an island,
daydreaming – Dry Tortugas, Gulf of Mexico]

ACROSS
THE BONES
OF MY
MEMORIES

THE PORTRAIT OF AN ARTIST

ELL, I'M IN NASHVILLE, TENNESSEE my new hometown. I am attempting to establish some form of roots in my life after nearly two years of roaming the country. I have not written a poem or kept a journal in over half a year. I have so much bottled up inside of me creatively, I feel as though I could erupt a Mount Vesuvius sized display of colour at any moment. It feels very freeing, in a sense, to be here. I finally have a small cavelike abode to call home, a place all to myself after years of couches, floors and hotels. This week I painted the walls to match my current mood and the state of my personality these days. Various greys, reds and dark browns. In my bedroom, which doubles as my office leaving just inches to walk through, I painted the wall by my desk a shade of green

to promote creativity and growth.

I found a place that sold gallery wrapped canvases at a very reasonable price so I've begun working on a four foot by five foot piece. I'm basing it off of a piece of tattoo flash that I came across depicting a sacred heart with wings. I painted the base colours with acrylic and am currently making the heart come to life with oils. I love using oils because they seem to know how I see things in my mind's eye as my brush flows across the canvas. Painting with oils teaches me patience, the time it takes to dry to the touch is very lengthy. I've heard tale told that even pieces over a 100 years of age are still not dry. Makes me wonder if anything I create will still be around a 100 years from now.

Today it is raining, I suppose that is why my energy rose to get out, have a cup of coffee and write. My emotions are on high today, it must be the rain. I can feel fall wanting to paint itself across this span of the earth. This is the brink of my favoured time of year. Fall into winter. Why does the best never last? The span of October to January seems to fly by with no regards to my longing for it to stay. The holidays, Halloween, Thanksgiving, Christmas ... large consumption of great food ... desserts, the giving of gifts, the smiles, contentment ... the rain, the snow, the sounds – fireplaces crackling, rain on the

rooftops, the crunching of snow underfoot ... the smells –
wood burning, evergreen, spices ... o, Fall, come to my
doorstep, I welcome you with open arms, jackets and
scarves.

I am currently so wrapped up in focusing on what's
to come that I don't want to look at my struggles as of
late. Yet I should momentarily, as writing things out
brings clarity to the situation and helps sort out the files
in my mind.

My greatest struggle is one that has remained
throughout most of my days. After my sudden move and
search for a place to live I find myself in a deep cavern of
financial angst, unable to provide myself with any kind of
consistent income. I refuse to use credit as it seems to
always fester into a bigger problem when freelancing. I
feel that I am good at so many avenues creatively, yet I
can't seem to ever make enough money to do more than
barely survive with any of them. Perhaps it's because I
am just good at them and not great. My God, I've strug-
gled for so damn long. *Where is the end of the struggle and
the beginning of success?* I can handle life just fine when I
let the art and talents lay dormant and take on a normal
job. I've proven time and again that I can acquire a wide
variety of nine to five's and climb through the ranks gain-
ing a decent salary. I feel that any man can use his hands

to provide for himself, but where is the journey in that? To live and die only to have worked to live and die. For me, it'd kill me if I offered no contribution to bettering the world or provide people a means to feel happiness or an escape to an enchanting place to ease the mind. That'd be a terrible end, a waste of my life. I only want to be a light and an inspiration with all of the years gifted to me. There is so much I have to give, so much I want to see. The daily struggle to survive *and* live out my art battle constantly in my mind and overshadow my will to express freely and allow a full dive into my creative pool.

Having lamented about all of this, if I don't find a way to make a decent income with my arts in the next couple of weeks I will be forced to pursue a full time job in a stale environment – once again stifling my creativity and placing it on the shelf.

Against my better judgement, yet in full alignment with my heart strings, I decided to reconnect with H– and attempt my first relationship since my divorce just one year ago. I know better, I am not ready. I have not healed, but I care for her and enjoy spending time with her. Aside from the love I do feel for her, I think part of it is that she was there for me when I was desperately in need of something, someone, and she filled a temporary void that was left amongst a gaping hole in the aftermath of losing everything I called my life. Some believe that all a relationship is for is to fill a void. Yet, I think to myself everyday – *where could I be internally now if I chose to deal with this tragedy completely on my own instead of taking on a relationship, perhaps only for comfort's sake.*

We have been an item since July, per her insisting and my request of having a normal, non-dramatic easy going relationship – sadly, it's been nothing of the sort. I have found it so hard to seek out any moments for myself to breathe and find my way. I do feel a strong pull towards her, but with this relationship I struggle in more areas than one.

She has said on many occasions I am the man of her dreams. Which scares the shit out of me. She knows I lack any desire to remarry, and I may never gain that desire back, so I'm not certain what "dream man" carries that charming quality. With her it's together on the road towards marriage or nothing at all, not even friendship.

I've not fully developed how I should now approach the sexual area of a relationship without, and on the other side of, marriage. After having been brainwashed with only one way to look at sex my entire life, I am now forced to live outside the scope of what I was taught. The church and the Bible leave absolutely no answers for this, as if it's not an option. This has been a taxing issue with us as well.

I am a soul that strives to better itself constantly. I never want to settle, I am always pushing myself to break through to the next level. It is part of that desire which proves to be a bit of a weakness at times. I get so down on myself for not improving in the most obvious of areas that I see need it. But with everything there must be balance, give and take, I can't live both my life and hers. I sit in a large bowl of limbo lacking direction but seeing the end of this relationship drawing nigh.

As I attempt to handle all of this madness, attempt to crack the mold of what is normal, I seek out the next breath of fresh air. Be it in a falling leaf, a raven overhead singing to me or the passing scent of a distant sweet memory. Either way, the future is a bright white light.

THE DEATH OF THE HUNDRED
YEAR DOORKNOB

 WAS SITTING IN MY OFFICE WORK-
ing diligently on a project due the
following morning. I paused momentarily to make a phone call then
proceeded to check my text mes-
sages and correspond with a few that I had missed, the
normal distractions of the twenty-first century. The time
was roughly 8:30 p.m. Mid-text I heard a thunderous
noise outside that rattled the door to my home office, it
sounded like a helicopter hovering closely overhead. Curiosity took the best of me, I set my phone down and
poked my head outside to see what it was. I saw nothing
beyond scurrying furry creatures as I walked further out
onto the sidewalk to gain a better glimpse at the sky;

turning back just in time to see the door shut behind me. I didn't realize that the door was spring loaded, but that's alright because I never spun a lock on the handle – as there isn't one. I grabbed the door knob to head back inside and to my despair it was locked tightly shut.

This house is 100 years old and constantly plays strange tricks in the night. The office door to the outside only has one lock, a small peculiar slide latch on the inside. The handle itself has neither turn-lock on the inside nor keyhole on the outside, and it isn't the push-in-to lock of some bathroom doors. It's merely a simple knob from 1892.

So there I was, stranded. I made the rounds trying the other two doors and checked every window confirming that, yes, they are all double paned and sealed from the inside. Having nary a flashlight or match I headed down under the house into the dirty, creepy basement. I had the thought of pulling one of the air vents out in an attempt to squeeze myself through the hole in the floor ... until my imagination played the result of that out for me, complete with the neighbors hearing freakish groaning coming from the basement. Not a story I wanted to be a part of. The last time I was in this basement I shook hands with 62 spiders and a dead rat. I wasn't in the mood for their company tonight. With a deep sigh, and a growl, I left the basement and headed above ground.

There I was – in my boxer shorts, sleeveless t-shirt and house slippers. I decided that all options were exhausted so I started walking. No neighborly lights were on so I continued up to West End to visit one of the stores and see about using their phone to call a locksmith. I made it past the church just as a policeman was veering onto the side road. *An answered prayer*, I thought. Flagging him down I asked if he had the number for a locksmith. He said, "Where's your car?" while looking at my boxers with a raised eyebrow. I replied, "Parked next to the house that I'm locked out of." With that he said I could walk back home in my cute little slippers and wait for the locksmith, he would phone one. I made it all the way back before the same officer drove up. *Thanks for the ride, didn't know you were headed my way*, I mumbled under my breath. He informed me that he called Pop-Lock and they would be on their way, shortly. Walking up the drive I heard the church bells chime, it must have been 10 or 10:30 p.m. I didn't pay attention to how many bells rung out. There I sat on my little concrete bench looking in on my cozy home as it grew colder and colder.

I attempted to use my time occupying my mind with things that were positive. I tried to see it as a break from work and tried to avoid thinking about all of the negative that has been surrounding me as of late. The bitter cold stifled my attempt, but I gave it a try. I began designing the landscape in my mind ... some flowers there, a few here ... The temperature must have dropped twenty degrees as I began to get really cold, teeth chattering cold, which made me think of how quickly Christmas was approaching. I began decorating the front yard, choosing where to hang lights ... what trees and bushes would look great lit. How great it would be to have family over for the holidays. The wonderful smells of the season ... baked goods, wood burning in the fireplace ... pine trees ... the various scented candles. Then the church bell tolled again. This time I lent my earn fully to the counting.

One ... two ... three ... four ... five ... six ... seven ... eight ... nine ... ten ... eleven.

The wind began to pick up quite a bit, I tried to huddle up and sit near the door but the ground was damp and my back aching. Just then I heard the same noise that rattled the door to begin all of this nonsense. With it came a lengthy train whistle again and again. The culprit was a train. There must have been tracks much closer than I had originally thought to be able to shake the ground this much. I was hoping the fox with the large whispy tail I had seen running through the front yard last night would appear again tonight and keep me company. He must have been inside his den being warm and fantastic. Lucky fox.

Time continued its slow creep around the dial. Just after midnight I saw my twenty-something neighbor pull into the drive. I approached her in the least creepy-guy-in-his-underwear way possible as she was saying goodbye to the friends who dropped her off. I introduced myself then informed her that I had a very strange request. My teeth were snapping together as I asked if she had an old sweater or a blanket that I could borrow until the locksmith arrived. She laughed, "Sure!" As I began to wait by her door she insisted that I come in. After realizing how long I had been waiting out in the cold she said, "I've got news for ya, the locksmith isn't coming." I feared she was right and let her phone another company. She opened the yellow pages and began thumbing through the locksmith ads, dialing up one that boasted, "15 Minutes or Less!" She gave them the address and I started to walk outside with the pink blanket I was lent. She requested that I sit on her couch and watch TV with her until the locksmith arrived. To pass the time we laughed at the television and threw questions back and forth to break the ice. I exuded a wonderful first impression as I looked like hell froze over curled up on her couch in a bright pink blanket, three days unshaven with tousled hair – sporting my boxer shorts.

At 1 a.m. she finally received a phone call from tonight's lottery winner. He had arrived in all of his smoke stench grease-ball glory. We made the rounds trying to see which door would be easiest to break into. He then mumbled that he would have to drill out the lock. Sounded real tough. He made me sign the bill first, as I read it I about fell right out of that bright pink blanket. I vehemently vocalized, "You've got to be kidding?!?" He said nothing. I knew he was grinning under that blank cockeyed stare. I began thinking of all the ways I could break in on my own with repairs costing less than one-hundred ninety-four dollars and nine cents. I could have busted through the basement floor, come through the drywall in the sealed off stairwell ... broken a window with my elbow ... Finally, I surrendered. Signed my name on the dotted line and let the jack-wagon proceed. On what planet is one hour considered "15 Minutes or Less!"? He drilled once on either side of the key-hole and *POP*. The door flew open.

And I lost two-hundred dollars.

I went inside, retrieved my debit card, brought it out and told him he could punch me in the face while he was at it. As he was leaving he had the audacity to say –

"Have a good night."

I took another deep breath and walked inside. Sitting at my desk I looked at the work I had left six hours earlier to investigate a noise, curiosity killed the cat. Things could always be worse. I could have been hit by the train that I heard.

I went over to my satchel in the corner of my office where I had two spare house keys that I bought just before I was in a car wreck a few days prior. I have a system with my car and my house so that this doesn't happen. I can always get into my car and with that I can always get into my house. But not today, today I'm in a rental car because my car is in the shop. In my car is a house key to my old home which would have been replaced by this new key if that woman wouldn't have turned left in front of me.

Could life make any more sense? I sat and thought of all of the other things I could have done with that money, like we do when the unexpected expense bites us. But it's gone. One more deep breath and I was over it.

I took one of the spare keys and found a place to conceal it outside then taped up the hole in the door where the hundred year old handle once lived. I wrote a quick thank you note on a card, sealed the envelope and placed in under the windshield wiper of my neighbor's car. Without her I would probably be frozen to the side-walk stubbornly waiting on Pop-Lock. As every story needs a moral I will spell this one out for you: *Always wear pants when seeking out noises in the dark.*

THE MEMORIES IN THE TREES

ODAY I WAS REMINDED IT IS THE little things that bring me peace and a spark of joy. I was busily running a handful of errands that needed to be completed as soon as possible. Turning off of West End into a somewhat secluded neighborhood I paused as I saw an elderly man, around 70, walking up to a tree, earnestly holding a camera in his hands. He was slowly snapping off pictures of this tree, which was stocked full of bright white flowers, rivaling the white of his hair. With each photo he would pull the camera down, look intently at this moment frozen in time and smile. Genuine, pure – uninhibited.

It always fills my heart with contentment when I see someone recreationally taking photos. I smile at the simplicity of it and seem to receive as much joy from it as they do.

Continuing down the street I thought about why he was taking photos of only that tree. I enjoy creating my own back-stories for scenes played out in front of me, understanding full well that I will never know their actual reality. Could he be reminiscing about all of the years spent around that tree with loved ones? Could he and his wife, who has now been gone for some time, have planted that tree together? Maybe that was her favourite flower and every year when it bloomed they would sit under the tree together and share the moment. Or, she would pull some blooms from the branches and place them in a vase on the dining room table. Or, perhaps he was just out for a walk and was so thankful for another day he simply wanted to capture a piece of its beauty.

Whatever it may be, I must pay more attention to the simple things and the memories held in the arms of the trees.

[Date unknown.]

A POLAROID

STEPPED OFF THE BUS IN FRONT OF
Grand Central Station as small clus-
ters of snow began to fall, sticking
to my eyelashes. I could feel the energy of the city beneath my feet. It
breathed like nowhere else I had been, the pace, the subway and the cultural cornucopia – a constant source of
inspiration. Always on the move, the rolling city gathers
no moss.

It felt good to be back. As I strolled up Lexington
Avenue I began studying the faces of those who passed
me by, each more intriguing than the last. I created a
backstory to match every face I met, filing them away as
a detective his evidence. I ducked into a subway terminal
to purchase a week pass; allowing me to stow away a few
moments of warmth in the crowded station. On my way

out a vendor gave me a kind and contagious smile – free of charge. It reminded me of a friend back home, a smile so bright that she warms the room. I smiled back with a nod and made my way out into the chilling air. I passed by a blind person – that made three in the last ten minutes – each walking with a cane in one hand and the arm of a friend in the other. True compassion. I don't know that it was completely circumstantial, I liken it to when one thinks about purchasing a vehicle, or makes the purchase, and begins to see that same model pop up everywhere on the road. Or, when you meet a beautiful and charming woman who strikes your fancy and you catch resemblances of her in those who pass you by in the weeks that follow. At any rate, since my brush with temporary vision loss I was aware and said a prayer for the ease of their struggle.

Breathing in the cold air I took to the charm of the city. From corner shops with their baked goods on window display to the delivery men running out of soup stands and Asian markets to jump on their bicycles and rush off to satisfy another customer. Flower shops seemingly on every corner displayed a wide variety of colour and life as bright as spring, even in the dead of winter. Fruit stands, hot dog vendors – buildings telling stories of old. I took the long route to my destination so as to receive a bit more of the city along the way. I didn't mind the blistering cold all that much. Still, I kept to the subway grates attempting to catch the rising heat taking its form in steam. Soon I arrived at Fifth Avenue. Taking a left I was surrounded by ritzy storefronts and high society hotels laced with faux gold. I laughed under my breath at how time can change a man. I lacked any interest in seeing the latest in fashion or design – I sought only one thing, Saint Thomas Church.

As I walked up its steps a homeless man was to my right taking to the stairs, bundled in jackets and using his cardboard proclamation to shield him from the unforgiving wind. I told myself that I would make a point to converse with him on my way out. I swung open the heavy wooden door. As it shut behind me it whisked away the city. Inside all that could be heard was the echo of footsteps and the occasional low rumble of a passing train below. I loved that the city was breathing at a runners pace yet inside all was as calm as a baby in the womb. I made my way down the aisle, past grain-bin sized pillars made of stone and underneath low hanging candelabras the span of chariot wheels. Entering a row of cold wooden pews I pulled out the kneeler and laid claim to my sanctuary.

An hour passed. The door felt heavier as the wind

outside made haste through the streets. The man was still huddled on the stairs. I approached him, took a seat and introduced myself. He obliged. "They call me C." Just a letter in a world that is at times full of too many words. I shared with him my bottle of water and a candy bar I had picked up on the go at Grand Central Station, as I hadn't eaten a thing all day. We discussed many things and he shared with me the woes of his life. He explained how badly he wanted to try and retain his CDL so that he could drive a truck again. We discussed the state of the economy and I asked him how he was holding up through the winter months out on the street. I left him there with a handshake and a candy bar. As I walked away I said a prayer for his well-being. There were traces of dishonesty surrounding him and his stories. Nevertheless, his soul was equally as important as the most saintly on earth.

Walking down Fifth Avenue towards Central Park I continued to collect inspiration from the faces I passed, the eyes I met and the life the old buildings gave. I took all of these and stowed them away – someday I will use them to create stories and visions that are all my own. These are the moments I live for. This is the part of life that makes the in-between bearable. Each day brings me closer to making a little more sense of my time here amongst the living.

[Thurs., 4 March 2010, penned at 12:25 a.m. – New York City, N.Y.]

REFLECTIONS OF A PASSING STORM

AM WRITING TONIGHT FROM Phoenix, Arizona. It is nearly 11 p.m., and I am sitting on the back deck at the home of a family friend. There is a strong breeze blowing across the trees, but for the most part it's rather quiet aside from the wind and a stray car. My companion this late June evening is a giant dog named Wallace. He continues to run in the yard chasing the wind for thirty seconds at a time then return to my side to lather my leg with spit and make sure I know he is still here.

I have been blessed tonight with one of my favourite things about this valley, the smell of desert rain. There is nothing like it. It is a sweet mixture – one part dirty earthiness, two parts freshness. They say we will be getting a downpour at some point tonight. Which tickles me a bit, after six full days here experiencing 110 degree temperatures I finally may get to enjoy desert rain again – it's been a dry spell. As my life has. Years of dry hot desert air before a beautiful thunderstorm and an onslaught of rain. I've yet to experience the fullness of a refreshing rainstorm in my life, but I know it's somewhere out there waiting for me to catch up with it. Knowing that I will reap as I sow is what keeps me going – keeps me giving all of my pursuits one-hundred percent. That and staying around for my family are what keep me breathing.

While in Phoenix I was able to lay out the piano parts and a few synth tracks for one of my new songs at the Famous Army Studio. Siege and I also tracked a haunting cover of a tune I've always loved. *Sour Times* by Portishead, lyrically enticing and emotionally stirring. I played a bit of lead using Kyle's Les Paul-rip, threw down a bass line and created the piano parts with my freshly discovered piano playing ability. In the next day or so Siege will lay his superb turntable skills across the track and we will talk back and forth about the mix till it meets satisfaction. It's a mite dark but satisfactory.

Tomorrow, around 4 or 5 a.m., I will head up Interstate-17 taking that oh-so-familiar fifteen hour drive into the Rocky Mountains, which is the current home of my immediate family. I only have a few short days in Colorado then it's back to Nashville for a couple weeks before I head out for spot date gigs in July. These summer days are filling up fast.

Wallace has just shoved his nose under my journal and laid his head on my knee, keeping watch of the darkness for us. It's amazing what a fantastic companion a dog can be. I scratched him behind the ears then picked up my pen.

Tonight my heart beats deeper. Tonight it's an old scar making it's way back from the past. Tonight the wheels are turning into heavy words on this page. Thoughts of love and loss bound to and fro in my head. Mostly feeding off of what my heart is feeling these days. The last time I was at this particular house was just over three years ago. I had dealt with a most tragic loss, one I would with a clear mind say was worse than death. Sitting in the living room, where I had sat those three years ago, I played out in my mind exactly how the conversation went amongst four caring adults twice my age. I could see myself sitting in that chair weeping uncontrollably with deep loss, longing and confusion. I removed myself from that moment and saw myself as I am today, sitting in that very chair. Things are different now. The sting still exists, I believe it always will. I believe, as mere human beings, pain never truly goes away. It is how we deal with that pain that makes or breaks us. It is a process that I have learned, the hard way. How else does one truly learn? Feelings are tricky. Situations arise and feelings shout much louder than reality. In that moment when emotions are high we *feel* as though we will never survive, never love again, never find the way out.

I have learned to remove feeling long enough to dwell in my mind with peace and think clearly through the situation. Knowing I can handle anything by removing feeling and emotion temporarily has helped me immensely. I am an incredibly sensitive person. And not just in ways of being emotional. I am very in tune with my surroundings. I can see and sense things that baffle others. Being sensitive definitely has its downside. But the upswing with the right relationship makes it worthwhile. Not to mention the amount of heart-sewn art that pours out of me. Taking its form via painting, writing ... music. I believe we go through experiences not only to grow and expand our knowledge of life but to be able to help others along the way.

While sitting at lunch with a friend this past week I began to open up briefly and discuss some of my experiences with love and loss. After much conversation this person looked me in the eyes and professed, "Cory, Cory

"... it seems you wear your heart on your sleeve a bit too much." I can't deny her statement. It is true. I question how else one would love, or find true love without that approach. If I play the catch and release game until walls are broken down and intense levels of intimacy arrive there is nothing left but to display my heart on my sleeve. As long as both parties take this journey together it is a very healthy start to a loving relationship. The problem arrives as one removes the emotional connection and begins a pattern of rejection. Selfishness can steer the prettiest of ships directly into an iceberg. When commitment is involved, spoken or unspoken, a selfish turn can destroy what was a beautiful beginning and leave a pool of pain. At what point do I decide this is not healthy for me, I should pack up and move on? If beauty is found in the beginning – a look, a smile, a piece of one's heart exposed long enough to catch a glimpse of what could be – do you hold onto that or close the doors to your heart to avoid a deep wound. I'm making these notes as a reflection, I surely don't have the answers tonight.

I read a plaque on the wall inside this house that displays the scriptures from I Corinthians, chapter 13. All of the things that true love is. I am left baffled by the last, love never fails. It doesn't? So what it's saying is all the love I experience that does fail isn't really love. This is meat I chew over and over and can never seem to swallow. I know in every relationship I have been in I love with absolutely all of me. I hold nothing back, treating the relationship as though it's the most important thing on earth. It's how I was created and for the most part it comes naturally. I know how I would like to be treated and respond as such, using information I learn about her needs along the way. I will say I have never experienced this fully in return. So am I to stop looking, stop loving? That's probably not going to happen.

With each love and each loss I learn a little bit more about who I am. There are times when I reread the script of a relationship and find no err in my ways. There is nothing I could have done differently. I have to realize what I want, wants me not. What I need, needs me not. Need is just a stronger sense of wanting. Many say one shouldn't need anyone or anything. Yet for me need is just a way to express that I crave it more passionately, more fervently with more vigor. Love, The Beatles wrote, is *all we need*. I believe the opportunity for true love exists for all of us. Whether we find it or not in this world painted with free will is another story – one without an ending.

I live thinking one day true love will fall out of the sky and smash me into clay. Until that day comes I will have to write a few sad songs, a few somber poems ... who am I kidding, a mountain of sad songs and a mountain of somber poems. Unfortunately in this world it can be the most relatable comforting thing we as humans cling to. It's why it is easier for me to put on Radiohead's *Creep* and connect immediately – as opposed to putting on U2's *Beautiful Day* and having it take a few moments to get there emotionally, telling myself everything will be alright.

Three years ago in that chair I was told to not give up on love, on God, on the commitment I made under the heavens. I was told the same things that brainwashed me and forced me to continue down the road to tragedy six years prior. The best thing I ever did was sit there in that chair and make the decision that enough was enough. I do believe it was the first time I ever felt a tinge of confidence in myself. It was the beginning of my new life. One void of the bullshit. I'm doing just fine out here on my own. In fact, I've never felt better.

I find it so peculiar and telling how throughout the twenty-eight years that I served and lived the way the church and the rulebook told me to, I would battle suicide constantly. I never felt I was good enough for anything, night after night I would lie in bed and say out loud, "I just want to die, I can't take living anymore,

God take me home." Albeit it wasn't just the church, years of being belittled and told I was nothing and worthless added to the suicide equation. But since making the decision in that chair ten feet away from me I am now fully recovered. I've not felt that way since I found my true self. My true worth. I wake up with a smile. The smallest of things bring me the greatest of joy. Life *is* so worth living, and I love it.

As I am about to close this journal Wallace is still sitting right beside me, accepting me for what I am. Gifting me a loving snout, eyes filled with kindness and a pure heart.

[Thurs., 26 June 2008, 8:03 p.m. – Phoenix, Ariz.]

LOVE ADVOCATE

AST WEEK I VISITED A SOMEWHAT normal haunt of mine here in Nashville. I hadn't been back since before Thanksgiving – quite an elongated spell. It's not that I had chosen another place to frequent when getting out of the house, it's just that I stopped getting out of the house. I can be somewhat of a recluse, the hermit syndrome overtakes me – it is easy for me to stay home for lengthy amounts of time without realizing how long it has been since I have been out. Working for myself out of a home office, and writing most of my music there, affords me that privilege and also that hinderance.

I sat down around 1 p.m. after ordering a meat and three, pulled out my headphones and hit play on my iPhone – choosing a random playlist. *Love to Be Loved*

by Peter Gabriel began to play. An emotional response is unstoppable anytime I hear this song, even when sitting in a crowded haunt eating eggs. I did have sunglasses on, although it was overcast outside. Not because I think I'm Corey Hart but because my eyes are very sensitive to being in an over-lit environment. I let go right there among a large crowd of people while wearing lime green headphones and sifting through my food with a fork. This is the power that love has over me. It's the reason I'm here. Not just to find true love, but to learn how to love others and how to receive love. It's something I try to portray in every piece of art I create, so that someday the emotion and love will penetrate the coldest of hearts. If any song embodies who I am and the honesty I wish to exemplify it's that one. No song has ever resonated so deeply into the core of me. The world stops when I hear it.

The beauty of music is that it can express so much for each of us and there is a piece of individuality in every song. It is given by the artist to do just that. To relate. To make it your own. I was first introduced to this song in such a vulnerable state. Sitting in a room with two new friends. We three were sharing our experiences with love and loss, all of us having a kinship in some respects to the depth of loss. Although each story was different, a bonding was taking place. They had both leaned on this particular Peter Gabriel album, *Us*, as a way to heal and now they were passing it on to me. We all sat eyes fixed on the floor as we listened to this song. Somewhat of an elevator moment. No one knowing where to look or what to say, but we were all in it together.

I left that night realizing I had been granted a gift. A small piece of my healing was to be received through this album. Shortly after arriving home I purchased *Us* on iTunes and sat attentive all the way through allowing it to work its magic on my heart and soul.

The fact that music holds power is all the proof I need to keep sharpening my skills – to keep crafting my art. Until I pass, I must keep learning and growing – knowing it can never be mastered gives me the freedom to take my time with it, allowing the music I create to come directly from experiences so it can be felt, not fabricated.

Although I may seem to be avoiding love by choosing to remain single for such a wearisome period of time, I am truly one of love's greatest advocates. And most days, I still believe.

[Date confidential.]

A FILM WITHIN A FILM

HILE THE WORLD SLEEPS, I WRITE. So many thoughts are buzzing through my head. I needed to grab this pen and attempt to capture them – like a fly to flypaper. Once I finish writing, my hope is the buzzing will end. I discard more writings than I keep; which is fine, because no one should keep dead flies.

Some days I just can't seem to write enough and there are other days when I pick up the pen and it all goes black. I can't seem to find the lens cap to remove the darkness and draw a crisp focus.

Since the days of my youth I've wanted to be a cow-boy, an astronaut, a football player, an animator, a rock star, a film star and so forth. Tonight I was pushed to add another profession to the carousel of desire. Director.

Call it dreaming big or call it self-torture, either way I can't stop doing it to myself. Tonight I was invited to a private screening of a film that has yet to be released. The film was *Gangs of New York*. It was quite a big tadoo – a Who's Who event in Hollywood. A handful of the actors and crew were in attendance as well as famed director Martin Scorsese, who sat directly in front of me. It was quite a trip to watch a film of this magnitude with the director sitting three feet from me. Following the film he graced the audience with a Q&A segment. Very easy going fellow, down to earth in more than just stature. I was mesmerized by how one man's idea could erupt into such a masterpiece. Of course, I wanted to speak at length with Scorsese but resisted appearing as a bumbling idiot, with little knowledge of the craft, and settled for a brief exchange instead. I can't say enough about this film, so I won't attempt much. Daniel Day-Lewis was hauntingly perfect – the soundtrack so moving – the scale and imagery dirty, yet divine.

While waiting in the wings to enter the theatre I was drawn to take notice of a mysterious ethereal girl. She was gorgeous. She wore a long black overcoat with a hood and a white scarf around her neck. Her hair was jet black with jagged bangs. Short bangs, trimmed above her eyebrows. The kind of girl you'd want to cast as the love interest in your music video just to play opposite her; the kind you'd fall for in an instant without even the exchange of names. It's quite peculiar to remain in the same proximity with someone you feel drawn to, for hours on end, without speaking. Exchanging nothing but glances.

She sat in the same row as I did during the film, about 20 people or so to my left. I attended the screening with a new female friend who was already heavily hinting an expectance of things to develop into more than a friendship – continually grabbing my knee, touching my face, and so on. I had all but forgotten that I was there with her once I made eye contact with this mysterious ethereal girl.

The night came to an abrupt close following Scorsese's discussion. The girl I was with was very eager to leave. I felt like it was all I could do to keep her from pulling my clothes off before we reached the parking lot. The mysterious girl lingered nearby watching me and waiting to see if I would make an escape. I refused to approach her out of respect for the girl I was with. It would have been rude and out of character for me. I never know where the line is or how to react when these dilemmas arise. The ensuing result is always the incessant buzzing in my head and an open-ended story to one day direct.

[Wed., 18 December 2002, penned at 2:58 a.m. – Hollywood, Calif.]

A FILM WITHIN A DREAM

HERE IS SUCH A FEEL-GOOD AT-
mosphere enveloping this local cof-
fee dive. I rather enjoy my visits to
Mel's, they should charge admission
for the people watching alone. This
morning my mind is swallowed whole by the dreams that
came last night; the girl who caught my eye at the screening visited me. Perhaps it was the long black cloak and
the way she carried herself – or, maybe it was the obscurity that allowed her entrance. If a happening doesn't
play out as you wished in reality, does your mind attempt
to recreate and deliver what might have been? If so, in
this case, my dream-conscious did a poor job.

The dream of her was very much like the reality of
her. It was dark, yet peaceful. She was around every corner – gifting me that same longing stare, a few entwined

with a half-smile. Time seemed to stop when our eyes connected. The closing piece of music from the film was the soundtrack to the dream. It was a U2 song, *The Hands That Built America*. Hauntingly fitting.

She spoke not a word. I followed around every building and into every alley yet still came up empty. I awoke feeling empty – with violins still echoing in my ear.

Why is it that the most talked about fish in the sea is the one that got away? It's the one you remember. It's the unsolved mystery. It's the buzzing in my head.

[Thurs., 19 December 2002, 10:15 a.m.
Mel's diner, Ventura Blvd – Calif.]

THE RUMOURS DIARY

HIS EVENING, FEELING A MITE BET-
ter and attempting to stave off a
semblance of cabin fever, I dotted
my eyes and drifted up the street to
a local watering hole where I would
sit a spell away from home to read, reflect and write with
fresh air in my lungs.

A local watering hole to most would be a raucous
dive on a street corner within the neighborhood, full of
charmed belching chums and American water-beer on
tap. Yet for my liking, a local watering hole is a quaint
place on a side-street with a sturdy candle-lit porch and a
bar overflowing with red wine and void of beer. *Rumours*, sitting quietly in the 12th South District, is a
stone's throw from the raucous.

I must admit my attendance here has been low this

past year. This would be the wine bar that my friends and I would spend many a nights deep in discussion; whether it be our dilemma with each of our current female of interest or the state of the world at present. Hours and glasses would pass until satisfaction of time spent under the night sky was reached.

This would also be the place where a beautiful foreign girl worked. At one point I expressed to one of my friends my interest in said girl. To which, under the influence of cabernet or not, he jumped at the opportunity to express this to the owner. Which resulted in the response I had expected. A resounding, "Oh, how cute. Yeah, sorry ... she's married." At that I sunk my head, and my friend raised a glass to his efforts.

Tonight, I brought a book and my small journal along. As I walked out onto the patio the woman working said, "Well, we're closing up for the evening."

I responded with the somber tune of, "Thanks, anyway ... "

Which she abruptly combated with, "Did you want a bottle ... or just a glass?"

"Just a glass, Ma'am."

"Well, in that case, have a seat ... what would you like?"

"*Chocolate Box*, please. Thank you."

I chose a table off in the corner with a seat facing the street. These past four years I have grown accustomed to receiving an uncomfortable feeling anytime my back is towards the entrance or the street. I suppose I'm sick of not seeing things coming. I pulled out my book, *The Rum Diary*, and my small package of clove cigars. A French couple was sitting in the opposite corner dining away on slender cigarettes; I knew I wouldn't disturb them. The only remaining patrons on the patio were two females sitting across from me. I politely interrupted them and asked if my smoking a clove would disturb them. Being allergic to standard cigarettes myself, I know how frustrating it can be when others smoke near you. The dominate of the two spoke, "Not at all, as long as you intend to share."

"Of course." I lit a clove for each and set away at my book, creasing each of the first few freshly purchased pages. I have oft thumbed through this book but never read it in its entirety. This time I would.

Pages one through five took me back to my time spent on Key West; as far south in the ole US of A as one could get. With that my mind drifted further yet – to the Tortuga Islands. Ninety miles north of Cuba, my small bit of Paradiso back in 2009. I reminisced of sleeping under the stormy skies with nothing but my fourteen-dollar sleeping bag; combating winds so swift they would literally move me across the sand. I recalled waking with the sun, stretching my limbs out over the water – eating my gourmet breakfast of beef jerky as I watched the gulls dive for theirs.

Oh to be back on that island, I said under my breath.

I thought of how funny it was spending all of that time keeping to myself on the island when there were four other people roaming about. The humorous part being that on the four hour boat ride back to the mainland I formed a brother like bond with one of the four. Having said no more than ten words to him while on the island, we didn't cease conversing the entire ride in. His name was Rourke, he and his girl Lauren chose the island for an adventurous getaway. They lived in New Mexico and his background consisted of a heavy intoxication of religion, not unlike mine. He was sent away on a two-year mission to live with a tribe of Indians in Northern Arizona. His mission being, convert the natives. In an odd twist of fate – they converted him.

Quickly realizing I was no longer reading *The Rum Diary* and was now watching my own life play back on a reel to reel in my minds-eye, I realigned my thoughts and set straight away back into reading the book.

Pages seven through 12 reminded me of my travels

to Buenos Aires, Argentina. I recalled being stranded at the airport in Atlanta as I had missed my flight. While the rest of the band went on, I remained after having had my Passport stolen; only to be recovered a half a day later by the FBI, who refused to answer any of my questions. I thought of how I finally arrived at the *Ministro Pistarini International Airport* in Buenos Aires after a 12 hour flight and equal hours of red tape. Once on the ground I searched high and low for the concert promoter who was nowhere to be found. I used what Spanish I had left in the memory bank from growing up in Phoenix and taking two years in high school; it was the growing up in Phoenix that got me where I needed to go. I remembered walking about late at night through the dark streets of the city wondering if I'd ever meet up with the rest of the band. At that point I felt invincible. I was alone in a foreign land without a care in the world. I could howl at the moon and no one would give notice. So I did.

Looking at tonight's moon, and laughing with a sigh, I led my eyes once again back to my book under the flickering candles on the porch at *Rumours*. The humid summer night made traveling back to those places easier still. Both brought forth the glistening of sweat on my skin and the intermittent cool breeze that followed.

I took another sip from my glass, sloshed it around a bit – then drank it down.

[Sun., 20 June 2010, 11 p.m. Rumours – Nashville, Tenn.
Rumours has since been leveled to make room for a hi-rise condominium.
There goes the neighborhood.]

EYES ATTACHED THROUGH LOOKING GLASS

OOSTERS RUN RAMPANT THROUGH the streets in this humidor of a country. This morning I awoke to the chaotic calls of quite a few. One in particular, perched beneath my window, seemed to have forgotten the last three notes of his morning revelry. While the others sang, *cock-a-doodle-doo* this fellow could only croon, *cock-a ...* Perhaps he was being dramatic. Or, perhaps he had been left with a malfunctioning brain after being run over by one of the eight million motorcycles on the streets of Quezon City. Or, maybe he, too, couldn't breathe through all of the pollutants swirling in the streets.

I slept quite well last night, all things considered. Before turning in I read a bit more of *The Old Man and the Sea* and returned to it this morning – digesting a few chapters at a time. Yesterday held fresh experiences for me, we took a bizarre little three-wheeled taxi to the bank so we could exchange our dollars for pesos. These taxis are motorcycles left by the U.S. Army following the war and have been rigged to house an enclosed sidecar. It's something out of *Mad Max*, like a metal milk carton with small windows welded over top of a motorcycle. Inside the city uniformed men were everywhere standing guard with assault rifles. Once outside of the taxi a man began yelling at me in Tagalog, the native tongue. I asked our interpreter what he was saying and was informed that he was telling me to: "Just go home!" How pleasant.

That evening we took a train into downtown Manila, once there we visited the home of a family who welcomed us in and cooked us a meal. Their home was directly under an enormous billboard on one of the tallest buildings in the city. The view from the top of the billboard was spectacular – truly an amazing sight. Patches of lush green gardens separated by poorly fashioned structures as far as the eye could see. Pockets of fog surrounded us creating the illusion of little islands floating under the sunlight.

While on the elevated train to Manila my eyes met those of a young Filipino girl, most likely around the age of 20. She was stunning. It was all I could do to keep from staring. I occasionally glanced her way and would catch her with eyes fixed in my direction. It was as if time stopped, or at least reduced to a slow crawl. I was snapped from my gaze by an elbow in the ribcage informing me that we had reached our stop. I departed the train and turned around to see if she was in view. It was the strangest of occurrences – we locked eyes through the looking glass of the train and remained that way until she was completely out of sight. With the train pulling off at what seemed to be such a slow speed the look seemed to last an hour – when in reality it couldn't have been more than two to three seconds at best. Before she left my sightline she smiled at me. It could best be described as a playful *I know what you're thinking, and I'm thinking the same* sort of smile. No words were exchanged. No touch or embrace given. Yet, I'd swear in that moment I believed in love at first sight. The feeling that came over me was one that words fail to match; something I hadn't felt in a long time. It seemed to have an existence beyond the dimension of human emotions. Unless she is my fate I am certain I will never see her again. It is these moments that leave a pull-tab in my memory book.

[Wed., 25 July 2001, penned at 8:00 a.m. – Manila, Philippines]

Scripting the Unscripted

ATE THIS MORNING I WENT TO THE grocery store. Milk, orange juice, frozen fruits for the blender. I stopped off on my way home at a coffee shop on Hillsboro. After receiving my drink I sat inside for a few moments, took in my surroundings and penned this thought: *just another day come and gone like all the rest, a speck of sand blown by the wind – taken where it's told.*

I inventoried the cast surrounding me playing the part of sitting in a coffee shop. Reading, scouring the internet, connecting via the smart phone. Quite standard, quite mundane. Yet, excellent role play by all. I missed the days of working on my book, writing in coffee shops. Too much to do in the office these days. I hoped that soon I'd get back to writing.

As I walked out the door I looked up to see a raven fly over my head. As it passed the tower of an adjacent church the bells released their midday song. All was quiet, save the tolling bells.

It is in those moments, which seem to be so scripted, that I know I am still here. Additionally, it is in those moments I know someone else knows I am here, and wants to make sure that I know.

I reached my car at the other end of the parking lot, strapped myself in and let out a sigh. Dialing in a playlist on my iPhone I pressed shuffle. *Almost Lover* by A Fine Frenzy began to soar softly through my insides as I backed out of my parking spot. Prior to passing the doors of the coffee shop a beautiful woman walked out in front of me crossing the street, making her way inside. Momentarily I had forgotten I was driving, forgotten I was sitting in a car.

Forgotten that I was still here.

All was quiet, save the song on my stereo and the horn of the vehicle behind me letting me know I *was* still here.

Timing is everything.

The rest, unscripted.

[Date unknown.]

THE MONASTIC JOURNALS

16 december 2011. written at 7:15 a.m.

HE LADY WHO MANS THE KITCHEN here at the abbey is bat-shit crazy. I walked into the kitchen to find breakfast and there she was, having a two-sided conversation with a can she was attempting to open. Upon seeing me enter she trained her beady eyes on me, watching every move I made – tossing comments for each. "Close that lid tighter, or we'll have to throw out tons of bread." I close it tight. "Now the other side. Do it!" I close the other side. She then proceeds to talk about all of the bread that has been wasted due to this lid that must be closed tight, on both sides. Perhaps the solution would be a better container system for the bread. But, who am I? I then prepare my toast in the toaster sitting just outside the

kitchen. I place two slices of rye in and slide down the timer. I proceed to place my small square of frozen butter atop the toaster, using its heat to give me something better to work with. I knew she would come out and say something; it was only a matter of time. Then I hear non-melodic humming approaching, so I quickly reach for the butter. Just as I do, she rounds the corner and begins her well versed butter-toaster speech. "Don't do that! I've found entire blocks of butter in that toaster from people doing that." She reaches past my hand and grabs for my butter. At this point I'm thinking it is no longer *my* butter so much as *the* butter. Regardless, she slops it down on my plastic plate. "There, it's plenty soft." I find a seat far away from the kitchen hoping another will enter to distract her. She stays in the dining hall, moving from table to table, fussing with each chair and each salt shaker.

"Are you leaving today?" I shake my head left then right. "So, Monday?" I shake my head left then right. "Well, people are leaving at 8 a.m. so it's going to get very noisy, we have to clean." Going to get? I think as I listen to her ramble on like tennis shoes in a dryer. I look at a placard affixed to the wall directly in front of me: SILENCE IS SPOKEN HERE. I go back to my coffee and toast as she flicks on a set of light switches. The room fills with the stale harsh white of a hospital, or a Walmart. I pull out my copy of John O'Donohue's *Eternal Echoes* and begin to take it in as I sip my coffee. At this point the kitchen lady finds someone else to speak with who is not on a silent fast. In my annoyed state I hastily finish my toast with the butter and gather my things. I find a dark corridor and make my way down and into a smaller room that appears to be cut into the earth.

Exposed rough granite and stone make up all four walls, and the only light in the room softly points to a large crucifix attached to the far wall. Approaching the table under the crucifix, I take out my book and set away to reading. As if on cue, I hear off-putting footsteps followed by non-melodic humming reverberating through the corridor, loudly approaching my position. She enters the room as the angels flee and flips on a row of fluorescent lights. "You need these on," she rattles off. I shake my head left then right and bury it into my book. It's rather ironic that in a monastery full of silent monks I can't get away from the one person who is far from silent. I imagine being around these non-speaking saints year after year has made the poor kitchen lady this way. God bless *Our Lady of Bat-shit Craziness*.

I try to shake it off. I need to find a rhythm in these days of silence – I need to make them count.

I am back in my 12 by 12 stone-walled room where I sit at a simple wooden desk with my books and a lit candle. This room holds a feeling of peace with a touch of comfort as I have hung a few of my scarves around the room, draping them over pictures mounted on the walls and across the desk filled with my books, journal and candles. The candle I have lit was a gift from a dear friend, a troubled soul. A kind and caring woman I have known since the tender age of 19. It is a soy wax candle titled Library. It emanates the most peculiar alluring scent. Betwixt the candle and the fresh leather binding of this journal I remain bewitched and charmed. I've always been one who is captivated by the memory held in a scent.

I am uncertain of the time as I have unplugged the clock, I can only guess it is around the hour of 10 a.m. I will know it is 12:15 p.m. when the bells ring out for sext, the monks' midday prayer and song.

After a light breakfast and a bit of reading I make my way to the visitor's center adjacent to the abbey. There, I spend over an hour studying practices and teachings of the Trappist, now Cistercian, monks. I take in a short film in a small theatre room sharing the early history and daily life of the abbey and its dwellers. Following the film

I peruse a collection of photos portraying the state of the abbey throughout the twentieth century. I was sad to learn of the destruction of the early design; beautiful faux gothic architecture complete with magnificent stone ornamentation and ominous arched enclaves removed in 1920 and replaced with stark white walls and ninety degree angled honey coloured woods. This was done to usher in the direct teachings of the Cistercian rule – to lead a simple life. It is tragic to see such beauty and art purposefully ruined.

I enter the small gift shop and spend a bit of time with their book collection and hand-crafted items. They must have over 40 books written by Thomas Merton. I painstakingly make my choice. Merton is a spiritual mentor in my life for well over a decade now. His minimal, yet powerful, writings in *Thoughts in Solitude* have been a constant companion. Merton was a contemplative monk who was unafraid to question or be transparent and vulnerable with himself. I decide to purchase *New Seeds of Contemplation*, a collection of reflections only briefly thumbed through. I also pick up *Dark Night of the Soul*, written by St. John of the Cross while he was imprisoned for attempting to reform the church. He is a sixteenth-century mystic who escaped his captors and then wrote his book. Much of his poetry was penned while in prison as one of his guards stashed a scroll for him.

I also purchase items to help the brotherhood of monks here at the abbey – two items crafted by their hands: Chocolate mint julep fudge, which will satisfy my ever-present sweet tooth, and a handcrafted wooden rosary. I attempt to taste the fudge but haven't a knife, which makes tactfully extracting a small portion impossible. I've had a rosary before that I bought at a small Catholic store in midtown Nashville, but it is cheaply made and constantly falls apart. Some Christians see the beads showing on my neck above my shirt and find it offensive I wear such a thing. I suppose because it represents pray-ing to Mary – something offensive to most Christians. I usually ignore the conversation when it begins. I am at-tracted to the rosary for its beauty, its sacred nature and its simplicity. I have from time to time on a meditative walk taken the beads from my neck and said a prayer for each. Conjuring up an image for each bead. Sometimes a family member, a friend, the state of the world, injustice or internal reflection. It is a rogue thing to do, but in the past five years there isn't much of me that is not rogue.

Today is void of a proper sky; low clouds hang just overhead and display no shape or change in colour. A seamless mid-grey tone blankets me. Yesterday held a touch of indian summer, gifting a pleasant 70 degrees.

Today, however, we are handed back our winter as the temperature lies just above forty. I return to my room among the monks' quarters and gaze out the window into the gardens where I watch a cloaked monk circle the brick walkway on a bicycle, stopping to take in the koi fish swimming in a small pond. I find it hilarious that he continually spits into the pond in an attempt to stir the fish. Soon after he peddles away I see the brightest red cardinal so wonderfully setting itself apart from the grey and dead winter grass, reminding me of the style I paint. The bells finish ringing in the hour of noon so I must put on something warm and make my way to the chapel for sext and then off to have my dinner – where I hope to commandeer a knife for this fudge.

written at 6:30 p.m.

I enter the church by way of the balcony, bow to the cross in reverence and take my seat. Sext begins with bells and the monks follow with a song for the lost and hurting of the world. From my perch I begin to study each monk as he stoically worships. Most of their faces hold many aging folds, each one a story – a year, like the rings of an old oak tree. Folds representing inward journeys taken. I have become an onlooker – a journalist – these past five years when it comes to any form of organ-

ized religion. I do certain things out of a lifelong reverence, yet on the whole I am merely an observer. No
longer a participant. I greatly admire these monks denial
of self and I whole-heartedly relate with the soul seeking
found in solitude with a contemplative nature.

As the bells ring out to close sext and usher in dinner I
move to the kitchen and find the same woman manning
the tile floor and stainless steel troughs of food. I think I
spot chicken fingers with a vat of honey-mustard alongside it, but turns out it is deformed fish sticks and a
strange pumpkin soup. As I begin eating and discover the
planks are, in fact, fish I hear my friend Jonathan's voice
in my head: "Be careful dude. Those monks eat a lot of
fish." For me to eat fish it has to be fresh and cooked in
such a way that it is void of that putrid fish stench, and it
also mustn't have a head with eyes attached so as to look
upon me from the plate and ask, with a sad face, "why
are you eating me?" I over-loaded my plate with fish as I
perceived it to be chicken. I fight my way through the
stormy sea of finless fish and with three pieces remaining
I can eat no more. I know *Our Lady of Bat-shit Craziness*
will be eyeing me as I eat and I wonder what she will
harshly say if I leave three sticks uneaten. If I could speak
I'd respond to her rebuke with, "I am leaving the three
uneaten fish along with your stale bread for Jesus to mul-

tiply." But I can't speak so I shamefully tuck the fish under a napkin. As if that isn't enough wastefulness on my part, I had grabbed a hearty piece of cheese while going through the food line, thinking that because it was made right there by the monks it would be spectacular. This turns out to be a grave mistake. The cheese smells so horrendous as it reaches my mouth I can barely chew without my gag reflex convulsing into a fit of rejection. The cheese now sleeps with the fishes.

I deliver my dishes to their proper waste bins and make my way through the labyrinth inside the abbey to my room where I begin studying *Dark Night of the Soul*. I take a small spoon out of my pocket and unwrap it from the napkin. Opening my fresh box of fudge I use the spoon to set free a small corner. The taste of mint julep within the soft chocolate is savory and divine until the robust finish of bourbon unexpectedly kicks me right in the jowls. I must admit that the bourbon does not distract me from partaking in twenty-five percent of the package of fudge.

I set the fudge aside and begin to take in the book. I am very interested in the forward, written by author Thomas Moore. He speaks of not using the term, "dark night of the soul," lightly. He said most never read nor experience the true meaning and circumference of this. At the end of a struggle people often claim they have gone through an ordeal and have come out happy on the other side – many take a degree of pride in this. I will expound further to say many vocalize their sufferings as to gain acknowledgement from others. Many seek to be validated for something they feel they have achieved by merely surviving. This can be argued as human nature, but I lean towards calling it a self-absorbed egotist personality. Moore said the spirit and the soul need not be separated. This sends me down a rabbit-hole of thought. Lately, I have jumped ship of any previous beliefs on life, death, spirit, soul and body, and have been looking at each under a new inner light. I have yet to draw a full conclusion as to what I believe. I have, however, found a few solid truths as to who I am and where I am at on this journey.

Simply because a belief is written as an interpretation and passed down through the ages doesn't make it an absolute truth. It is in the present we must distinguish between the self and the soul. The self adjusts to a difficult world, deals with passions and emotions and builds the personality, while the soul is vast in comparison, full of mysteries containing the high mysticism of contemplation and visions to the deep struggles with meaning and connection. I feel we are in a culture that convinces people the meaning of life is financial and psychological. But, in the very heart of a career decision, a painful divorce or the memory of abuse lie questions of meaning, purpose and value. Spiritual issues are being forged in these emotional crucibles.

Upon entering the monastery I made a vow to continue what I took away from my last stay, five years ago. A bi-way of denying the self. A need to pull focus away from daily troubles, issues, thoughts – the relationships, the search for a bonding mate, the finances, the creative undertakings, et all. Instead moving towards a pendulum shift to separate the spirit and soul from the previous and only draw focus to the enlightenment of these two facets of my being. Like clockwork as I write this I look up to see a book on the shelf in front of me: *There Are No Accidents*.

Hours later I find myself outside briskly walking the stations of the cross, taking in each one as I pass. At the end I found I am under a magnificent tree with a large low-hanging canopy of protection even in the dead of winter. Underneath the tree is a statue of Mother Mary holding the infant Christ in her arms. At the bottom of the statue I notice her bare foot stands on the neck of a serpent. I've always been drawn to iconic Catholic art, from paintings to sculptures – yet somehow I have missed the serpent at Mary's feet. The statue stands about five feet tall and is aging rather nicely, covered head to exposed toe with various moss and black soot. Surrounding her are various offerings, mostly crafted with nearby findings from nature – stacks of stone thoughtfully placed, twigs tied together with shafts of wheat forming a cross. Here I feel a calm peaceful presence that is almost unexplainable. I've never subscribed to the belief that the Virgin Mary holds any supernatural power or answers prayers on our behalf, but then again, I wasn't raised to believe this way. Perhaps I felt the grace of the monks and the sincerity of the countless prayers uttered here.

As the hidden sun makes its way to the horizon, the sky begins to break and the steady grey of the day begins to disassemble, giving way to a vast palette of colours. I sit in a neighboring graveyard against a marking stone and watch the sunset develop around me. In the silence I can almost hear the clouds separate. The falling sun began to escape me behind the foreground of a hill. I quickly make my way to the hill and climb to its top where a large statue stands. Together we look over a small valley and watch the darkness chase the colour away. In the blackness I feel my way down the hill and back to the abbey, just in time for supper.

It is the absolute perfect choice after coming in from a long stay out in the cold. Chicken and rice soup coupled with grilled cheese sandwiches and a side of pudding for dessert. It reminds me of the good times as a child when Momma would prepare the same. I am pleasantly surprised to find the previous kitchen lady absent and in her stead the sweetest woman with a welcoming smile and demeanor. She respects my silence and makes certain I have what I need. As soon as I finish my supper I enter the kitchen to load my dishes and set off to find a warm place to continue reading.

I find the monk's library a great place to study and focus. So silent my thoughts sound like trains passing each other through a tunnel. It made for a good practice of controlling my thoughts and finding my center. I stay for over an hour, reading and writing until the bells alerted final prayer. I quickly make my way to the chapel to observe compline, the seventh and last of the canonical hours. I do nothing but observe but can feel my innards longing to sing along with the drone pattern of the chanting Psalms.

written at 10:19 p.m.

I've been reading and writing in the library for the better part of three hours and have made a home of this table with found books of poetry – Rilke, Byron, Thoreau along with other books – *Dictionary of Saints*, *The Foun-*

dations of Mysticism to name a couple. From Rilke I soak in a beautiful piece, "This is the Creature," which I take as contemplation on being. In this piece the unicorn is imagined to have endless possibilities of being, yet only seems to be able to do so when looking in the mirror. From Lord Byron I love – "She Walks in Beauty," "Stanzas to Augusta," "When the Moon is on the Wave," "So We'll Go No More a Roving." And I also take in Thoreau's "Civil Disobedience."

17 december 2011, written at 8:05 a.m.

This morning in the early hours I awake with the thought: *What is pain when emotions are removed?* When feelings are taken away do we no longer know that the pain is there? Physical pain is the body's way of alerting the mind something is wrong, something needs your attention.

We must strive to separate the feeling, emotion, from the pain of the soul and heart. This is not a call to remove it altogether, rather to pull the protective shell away to look at the root. The core without the distraction of emotion. This is something that can only be done with a healthy sound mind that is fully present. To numb emotions so as to no longer feel the pain is not the answer here. Focusing on the way the pain makes one feel allows the root to remain covered, unexposed. Acknowledging the pain in its early stages, by spending a small portion of time with the feelings surrounding it, gives way to a soft approach to the root. In the same way a candle gives light to the walls of a cave. Dismissing the feelings would be like exposing the pain instantaneously to a hospital room full of fluorescent white light. Approach the pain softly, acknowledge the way it makes you feel, yet do not dwell. We must discover why the pain is there. Dwelling on the feeling would be like catching on fire and letting yourself burn alive simply because you are mesmerized by the way fire dances about your body and the colour it produces.

After acknowledgement – name the feeling. Respect that it was put there to alert you something has gone awry. After every feeling has been identified you are now free to investigate the exposed root. Here is where we should be spending the majority of our time and focus. When the human psyche is in pain the immediate response is always to get rid of it. I no longer want to feel this way, and more oft than not, I never wanted to feel this way to begin with. We can't give in to this response. We must always approach pain with the desire to learn. Pain is responsible for a large amount of the growth in my life. Those who appear the same as they were when you saw them last, years ago, are that way because they are pain deflectors. They deny themselves the experience by choosing a vice to numb over the opportunity for growth. If you spend any amount of time looking you will find these types of people are void of purpose in this life. And, sadly, with the vast amount of vices afforded society via technology, these people can appear to be the majority. The knowledge and wisdom gained through uncovering the mysteries of your pain at its root will be your reward.

I must briefly write about this vivid sleeping dream I had last night. The subject matter is my immediate family and paired things we've lived through with things that haven't happened, but I've always feared would. I can only ascertain this dream was formed by thoughts freshly left in the recesses of my mind as last week I had a lengthy in-depth conversation about all of these things with my friend Tait. Furthermore, it could be my senses disconnecting from my spirit, beginning with the most emotional and heaviest of my heart pains.

I slept with my fourth floor window cracked to be chilled enough to sleep bundled in blankets. This was a mistake as it was probably in the low thirties last night, if not colder. The surrounding earth is covered with a crys-talized coat of ice. I awake so cold I don't want to uncover and dress for breakfast. Eventually I force myself out from under the blankets and attempt to fire up the baseboard heater – it does not oblige. It seems out of commission, or in a contemplative state of being. I once again make my way through the labyrinth of hallways and stairwells finally revealing the dining hall. I hope to be greeted by the sights and smells of a hot breakfast. To my dismay it is the same as yesterday – cereal, toast and fruit. Dismayed yet grateful I pour myself a bowl of cereal and a cup of coffee and then bring my toast to the toaster and look around like a cat burglar for the kitchen lady. I don't see her so I set my square of butter atop the toaster. Just as I do footsteps come from around the corner. It is the sweet kind kitchen woman, she simply smiles at me and walks on. I am not paying attention as my toast pops out and like clockwork my square of now-melted butter slides into the toaster. I almost burst into laughter but catch myself by biting hard on the inside of my cheeks. I quickly unplug the toaster and fight the squishy square of melted butter with my spoon. I finally win the battle by dislodging and sending it flying into the neighboring garbage can. I sit, am grateful for my food and begin to eat. For a moment, I can't figure out why my cereal has a hint of butter.

Later, I return to the library. I devour books by Merton and dissect his "Message to Poets" from the book *Raids on the Unspeakable*. He has many beautiful thought-provoking lines of truth for the poet, yet I find myself questioning and disagreeing with a handful of his points.

I also came across a breathtaking piece written by Rainer Marie Rilke (1875 - 1926). It stirs such emotion I am compelled to write it down and vow to return to it when I am not shutting off the personality to focus on the soul and spirit.

> *Love-Song*
>
> *How shall I hold my soul, that it may not*
> *be touching yours? How shall I lift it then*
> *above to where other things are waiting?*
> *Ah, gladly I would lodge it, all-forgot,*
> *with some lost thing the dark is isolating*
> *on some remote and silent spot that, when*
> *your depths vibrate, is not itself vibrating.*
> *You and me - all that lights upon us, though,*
> *brings us together like a fiddle—bow*
> *drawing one voice from two strings it guides*
> *along.*
> *Across what instrument have we been spanned?*
> *And what violinist holds us in his hand?*
> *O sweetest song.*

I have two separate dreams this afternoon while taking a nap. They are both in black and white involving deep personal players in my life. From what I recall, writing now in a foggy state after just waking from them, the main character is a person that is both my ex-wife at some points and the girlfriend who was my first kiss at others. She seems to morph between the two. The ex comes to me distraught and tells me her parents were gone. "Gone?" I said. As in missing, kidnapped or ... dead? She alludes to the fact they ran off to commit suicide together in a pact – as if all other hope is gone. I tell her I will help find them. Somehow we connect with my sister who has her kids with her and we were suddenly searching for our parents. We find ourselves in our old neighborhood going door to door in search of them. At one point, my sister's youngest child starts walking off toward an abandoned house. I tell her no and demand she return to us. She doesn't listen, so I run over and grab her. She is very upset with me as I say, "you are not playing with that other girl over there – you'll disappear too." My sister looks at me. "There's no little girl over there, what are you talking about?" To which her daughter replies, "Yes there is momma, she's right there staring at us." She looks again and sees nothing. This freaks her out so I distract her by saying, "We must keep looking for Mom and Dad." There are other strange occurrences; like how we arrive at certain places as if they are in other dimensions. We have to believe and pretend these places are there and they will magically appear. We pretend we are walking down a vast ornate staircase, and then suddenly we are at the bottom of these stairs and in an entirely different area.

We run into an old neighbor whose face I recognized but couldn't put a name to. He is disillusioned as his family has gone missing. He keeps walking in circles repeating, "Wait, they'll be right back!" It is at this point my father enters the dream. There is heavy dialogue I can't recall. It's hard to explain the shape shifting that occurred, continually morphing my ex-wife into the girl I was with at 19. I awake in a momentary daze during this dream and fall right back to sleep, quickly entering the next. In this one they're both separate beings. I recall a few poignant pieces from this one. I am at a fancy low-lit location dressed very well. It is my first date back with my old girlfriend after more than fifteen years. Suddenly, my ex-wife shows up while I am waiting and begins to seduce me with sadness. The next thing I recall I am on a rooftop terrace eating dinner with my Uncle when I receive a phone call from, Justine, a friend whose voice I haven't heard in years. I walk down a flight of stairs after excusing myself and take the call. The voice on the other end is crying loudly and begins saying things like, "... I can't believe you would do this to me. First he did, now you!" I ask her what she is talking about and she said, "they have video of you with some skank at a hotel, how could you do this? You're going to get us kicked off the show, I'm sure everyone has seen the video by now." From what I gather we are both on a reality game show like Survivor. I want to tell her that it isn't just *any* skank but my ex-wife and she needs me, she is in serious trouble. But I don't say these things, I just keep listening to her cry and scream until I awake. And as I do, right in front of my eyes, crawling up the window is a bright red lady bug with four black dots separating my black and white dream from the grey sky.

I'm not going to take the time right now to decipher these dreams, I simply think they are a purging of the senses, releasing my fears and my pains. A mixture of that and the actual realities I am walking through. In just three weeks' time I am to visit with the girl I was with at 19 years of age, as we have recently reconnected.

After writing my dreams I grab my satchel for another walk in the gardens. This time as I stand with the statue of Mary, under the canopy of the giant tree, I notice a whole cigarette propped up carefully against her foot, the one atop the serpents head. I think about this. If one has enough belief to actually believe Mother Mary could help him/her with their addictions does that faith not hold power enough to make it so? Who am I to say these prayers fall upon deaf ears? I take time to soften the areas within that lay hold of previous beliefs and hardened ideas of what I thought I knew, or was told I knew.

I walk outside the gates and look up at this house of silence and am thankful this gate has nary latch nor lock. It remains wide open and ready to receive the seeking wandering soul. I grab a tree branch fashioned into a walking stick laying with others against the outer wall as I make my way off into the surrounding wood.

Eventually I return to the hill I visited the day before and sit in the blistering cold with the statue and watch the sun tuck itself in below the blankets of clouds, brushing each one with magnificent colour on its way down. As I wait and watch I take in the words of Thomas Merton in *New Seeds of Contemplation*, rereading lines to emphasize their import. The sun says goodbye to the day as the bells declare the beginning of vespers. I say goodbye to the statue and the sky as I make my way down the hill and through the wind into the safety of the abbey.

Upon entering I pull my journal from my satchel and pen this piece of poetry.

O Wisdom,
I seek you
I chase after you.
I lay awake all
Hours of the night, and
I beg of you —
Come lie with me.
Become one
With my soul
Consummate my desire.
Out of love
And not pride
Do I call upon
Your window,
Do I come
Rapping upon your
Door.
For if
By dawn
We are

Not one
The day is
Already doomed,
And I will
Chase away
The sun
And call
Upon the moon.
For in the shadows
You wait.
In the darkest crags
You grow.
O Wisdom,
I seek you.
And I will chase
After you
Until my heart
Beats no more.

— Abbey of Gethsemani, 17 december 2011

written at 8:30 a.m.

I will now break my silence. My hope is I have given all I was meant to give, and I have received all I was meant to receive.

It's a strange state to be in as I have become fully

aware of the depth of my being. I now know what it is to fully purge and separate my senses and spirit from one another, and furthermore from the personality or self. I have studied all I could study in these past five days and I sense that because of its enlightenment a different kind of journey has begun. There is much I will take from this – things I will never forget, things I will cling to and reflect upon. Knowledge I will own and wisdom that will carry me throughout my journey on this earth. I feel as though I have experienced, through contemplation and transference, a mountain high happening in my soul. There have been no emotions attached and no physical transformations – my self did nothing but surrender to a time of silence and study.

Returning to the daily grind of decision making and business is not something I am excited about, yet it is the path I have chosen to walk. The intensity with which I studied and sought was mentally exhausting as I tried to understand all I focused on. I know a majority of the studies were for the soul, thus depleting my body on all fronts. Solitude and silence I can and do crave from month to month, but to live the rest of my days in that state is something I could not do. I am quite taken by the strength of these monks to truly surrender all. The power of not speaking lies in the denial of self. When one denies the tongue the ability to speak the personality is shut down. When one commits to not speaking he or she takes away the self's strongest asset, therefore allowing the contemplative state to take form.

***

The way from here has become clearer, my steps need not be ordered as the timelines formed by the memories burned across the bones of yesterday. My life is my own to mold as windows and doors open along the road.

Driving away from these gates I welcome today with open arms, in anticipation of the future, what new marks I will make and the continuing evolution of my spiritual being.

ACKNOWLEDGEMENTS

O THE CREATOR, THANK YOU FOR gifting me the patience and purity to discover who you are to me. To my family, who I'm certain have been watching from the sidelines holding up giant question mark signs, thank you for your unending love and devotion. To the tried and true; Michael Bass, Jason Pugh, Chris and Laraine Gilbert – thank you for your steadfast loyalty. To Rourke McDermott, blood brother, thank you for showing me how to live under the sky. To my Nashville tribe, you've shown me what true friends are – much love to you. Rory White, may our late night chess matches filled with elixir and conversation live on until we expire. To the great Scarpati, thank you for working your magic on the photography for this endeavor, and most importantly – the grilled cheese sandwiches. Kevin Max, thank you for your friendship and the wrangling days which pro-

vided perspective to my unexposed mind on all sides. To my editor, Melissa Wyllie, it's been a pleasure taking these steps alongside you – may we murder the unnecessary "that" again very soon. Amy Neftzger, thank you for diving headlong into the water with me – *feet first, first time* is for the weak. Yes, I'll still take your calls if you take mine. To *The Frothy Monkey*, the perfect neighborhood haunt, many thanks for your warmth and support.

To the Muse – you continue to propel me further and further beyond the breach.

Proper acknowledgment to all of the following delights:

Those who help the helpless selflessly. Kindhearted strangers on the road. Patrons of my art. The Abbey of Gethsemani. Dry Tortugas. Monument Valley. Ocracoke. New York City. Caravaggio. Van Gogh. Burton. Depp. Hitchcock. Wayne. Luhrman. Poe. Yeats. Joyce. Wilde. Longfellow. Rilke. Neruda. Bukowski. O'Donahue. Shakespeare. King. Debussy. Mozart. Beethoven. The creators of Chess. The Twilight Zone. 60's Space TV. The Incoming Ship. The Green Hills baristas. The Smiling Elephant. Parnassus (saving the tangible). Ian White Tattoos. Tait. The Flipper. Comrad. Grey Knit Hat. Music. Spinach. Oatmeal. Cloves. Rum. Red Wine. I Ching. 11. 4. Ravens. Dead and Living Trees. Skulls. Fall. A.S. Anam Cara. The Sea.

Lastly, to you, reading these pages, thank you for spending your hard-earned coin to partake in my journey – I am indubitably honored.

goodnight, until then

when i die
in bed as i sleep
i pray ye – do not weep.

yet in the morn' when you find me
please lie beside and read
my favourite prose and poetry
from Poe, Longfellow and Yeats.

and i will ask of the one who reaps
to allow me a moment
of listening as you breathe
and read
ever so softly –
the words aloud to me.

[20 may 2012, the Observatory, 11:11pm]

Printed in the USA
CPSIA information can be obtained
at www.ICGtesting.com
LVHW091632020923
756761LV00062B/428